PENGUIN BOOKS
#KINDNESSMATTERS

The UNESCO Mahatma Gandhi Institute of Education for Peace and Sustainable Development (MGIEP), UNESCO's first and only Category 1 Institute in the Asia-Pacific, focuses on peace and sustainable development through education. The Institute operates on a global mandate (with specific focus on the Asia-Pacific region) and develops programmes that promote social and emotional learning (SEL); innovate digital pedagogies; and empower the youth to promote sustainable lifestyles, a culture of peace and non-violence, and an appreciation of cultural diversity.

On the occasion of the International Day of Non-Violence, 2 October 2018, UNESCO MGIEP launched an international youth campaign on kindness for the Sustainable Development Goals (SDG), titled '#KindnessMatters for the SDGs' to mobilize the world's youth to achieve the 17 SDGs through transformative acts of kindness, compassion, care towards self, others and the environment. These acts can range from a simple impulse to a well-planned, organized activity.

This movement promotes a culture of peace and empowers individuals/communities to take personal/community ownership/ stewardship of critical local issues all the way up to global goals.

#KINDNESS MATTERS

UNESCO MGIEP

unesco

Mahatma Gandhi Institute of
Education for Peace and
Sustainable Development

PENGUIN BOOKS

An imprint of Penguin Random House

PENGUIN BOOKS

USA | Canada | UK | Ireland | Australia
New Zealand | India | South Africa | China

Penguin Books is part of the Penguin Random House group of companies
whose addresses can be found at global.penguinrandomhouse.com

Published by the United Nations Educational, Scientific and Cultural Organization
(UNESCO), 7, place de Fontenoy, 75352 Paris 07 SP, France; the UNESCO Mahatma
Gandhi Institute of Education for Peace and Sustainable Development, 35, Ferozshah Road,
ICSSR Building, 1st Floor, New Delhi 110001, India; and Penguin Random House India
Pvt. Ltd, 4th Floor, Capital Tower 1, MG Road,
Gurugram 122 002, Haryana, India

First published in Penguin Books by Penguin Random House India and UNESCO Mahatma
Gandhi Institute of Education for Peace and Sustainable Development (MGIEP) 2021

Copyright © UNESCO 2021
Written by Stuti Agarwal and researched and curated by Carina Racine

ISBN 9780143447115

Book design and layout by Canato Jimo
Typeset in Goudy Oldstyle Std by Manipal Technologies Limited, Manipal

www.penguin.co.in

Contents

Forward

Kindness is defined as being considered friendly and generous. We foster and value these qualities in my family. In a world where you can be anyone, being kind is and should be the fundamental base of all actions.

In the words of my son Prince Noah, 'Kindness can take many forms and is expressed in different ways depending on culture, age and upbringing.'

The Covid-19 pandemic has highlighted the need for more kindness in our societies around the globe. The virus does not discriminate between who you are and where you are from. But the sad reality is that not everyone has the same access to medication and treatment even today. Kindness could be a tool for change, compelling countries to collaborate more and be kinder in sharing resources and knowledge, and formulating policies based on science, evidence and empathetic concern.

Furthermore, a humanitarian crisis is unfolding in Afghanistan, and a collective effort and kindness to those displaced is the only way forward.

During these times of unprecedented crises, this collection of kindness stories from around the world will help you rekindle hope. These are stories that have inspired me personally. Stories of human beings showing examples of what it means to be kind and receive kindness.

As a proud Patron for the UNESCO MGIEP #KindnessMatters Global Campaign, this book provides an inspiring illustration of what it means to be human.

Dame Tessy Antony de Nassau
Patron, #KindnessMatters Campaign
Former HRH Princess of Luxembourg
UNAIDS Ambassador
Co-founder, Professors Without Borders

Introduction

Greetings from UNESCO Mahatma Gandhi Institute of Education for Peace and Sustainable Development (MGIEP), where we see the need to contribute, help, support and belong as a fundamental predisposition in human beings, who are inherently kind.

Neuroscientific studies have shown that altruistic, kind behaviour engages brain networks associated with reward processes. At UNESCO MGIEP, we hope to capitalize on this fundamental biological need to build a new way to drive positive change. With that in mind, kindness is not defined by lofty stories; it exists all around us and needs to be celebrated in every moment of life because #KindnessMatters every day. An act of kindness by any person is a generous, deliberate gesture or action for self, others and nature. We launched the #KindnessMatters Global Campaign to gather stories of youth doing acts of kindness to create a positive culture of compassion. We wanted to show the world that every person's selfless acts mattered. This book documents that transformative power. With care being taken to focus on individuals of all ages, from all over the world, *#KindnessMatters* brings out stories of human interest that are unique, impactful and a testament to the positive and sustainable change people are able to create. These fifty stories are just the tip of the kindness iceberg.

Thanks are due to many individuals for their participation in this project, above all those who have agreed to share their story with us, those whose names are known and many anonymous ones working alongside them. Through her words, Stuti Agarwal was able to pay homage to these stories of kindness in an aspiring way. Moreover, this project could not have been possible without the support of the team at Penguin Random House India and the precious help of Smit Zaveri, Aditi Batra and their eye for detail. Each of these stories had to be found and selected, and this was only possible through the research and coordination by Carina Racine with the support of Abel Caine.

Thank you for spreading kindness with us!
Reflect. Empathize. Be kind.

Anantha Duraiappah
Director, UNESCO MGIEP

PERENNIAL

Rosemerry Wahtola Trommer
(United States)

Sometimes even a small sweetness—
a kind word, a kind act—

is robust enough to take root,
and though its perfume soon fades

and its petals wither,
the roots persist so years later,

when you least expect it,
there in a forgotten field,

or perhaps in your own well-tended yard,
you catch the scent of sweetness

and follow it until you find again
the fragrant bloom of it not at all

diminished by time. No, maybe sweeter
because it was forgotten.

Sweeter because with roots like that,
you now trust it will come back again.

* Curated by *The Alipore Post*

1

The City of Kindness

A YOUNG GIRL'S DREAM OF A CITY BUILT ON KINDNESS

United States

'Put your heart into kindness', the words curved with the yellow of the rainbow. A bright blue flower bloomed with hope underneath it. 'My wish is to help people,' said another note squiggled by six-year-old Natasha Jaievsky.

This was one of the many drawings that Edward Jaievsky discovered in his daughter's bedroom after she passed away in a tragic car accident in 2002. Each of her drawings featured a colourful rainbow. Each rainbow had, within its curves, a message of kindness. It was what the little girl wanted most from the world around her.

In the hope of honouring his daughter's memory and fostering the message of kindness that she advocated, Jaievsky decided to poster their hometown of Anaheim, California, with her banners.

Many pairs of eyes would see these rainbows plastered around the city, and City Councilman Tom Tait would be one of them.

Mr Tait recalls Jaievsky holistically telling him: 'In holistic medicine, you can either treat the symptoms or you can stimulate the body to heal from within. The same applies to a city. And I think that has something to do with kindness.'

The dialogue with Jaievsky and the message from his young daughter inspired Mr Tait to run for mayor with a kindness campaign. He would holistically heal the city from within and create a culture of kindness.

Mr Tait won the election and became Anaheim's mayor in 2010.

As mayor, 'Hi Neighbor' was one of the first kindness initiatives that Mr Tait implemented. This was a community-based programme that encouraged residents to get to know their neighbours and share kindness with one another.

The idea sprung from the understanding that in emergencies and disasters, when the first responders were stretched beyond their limits, it was the neighbours who helped each other out. In fact, New York University sociologists found that tight-knit neighbourhoods often fared better in terms of emergency and disaster preparedness. This is because a community built on kindness enjoys greater resilience.

The campaign led to many others, the most successful one being 'The Year of Kindness' that launched in 2013. After a meeting with the superintendent of the city's elementary school district, Mr Tait decided to ask the kids to create a million acts of kindness. 'And they did it!' Mr Tait smiles.

From simple acts of kindness, like holding the door open for someone, paying an honest compliment or helping parents with household chores, to bigger ones like planting trees and visiting senior living centres, each school amassed 40,000–50,000 acts of kindness, and each child contributed 40–50 to the total.

'It changed the DNA of the school,' Mr Tait recounts.

The calls of indiscipline to the principal were cut by half. As were suspensions and cases of bullying. And this was in one of the toughest schools in the city! So large was the impact that even the Dalai Lama took notice and said that kindness, starting in school, was the path to world peace.

The importance of kindness in boosting a more harmonious local community is profound. During Mr Tait's mayor days, the city of Anaheim saw a decrease in youth crime rate and addiction problems, and an improvement in public safety. Most importantly, happiness and kindness became a growing sentiment.

Tom Tait is no longer the mayor of Anaheim, but what he started continues to grow under the City of Kindness, which is a platform to exchange ideas to spread kindness.

Of the many projects under its wing, there are simple ones like 'The Free Flowers Project', whose mission is that one should spread kindness to strangers by handing out free flowers in the local community; powerful ones like 'Empowering Cuts' that provide free haircuts to those who can't afford one; and ones that are all heart like the 'Kindness Closet' started by a fifth-grader to help fellow students who cannot meet the expense of new clothes.

From 2004, when Jaievsky first put up the banners, to 2011, when Mr Tait initiated the first campaign, and the present day, the message of kindness that Natasha sought to tell through her drawings has brought about great change in the fabric of not only the city of Anaheim but many other cities that have followed its example.

'Make Kindness Contagious', Jaievsky had written on all the posters he hung up. And making sure it spreads is the only way to peace and healing from within.

* This story was adapted from an article originally published on Goodnet.org, a kindness collaborator of UNESCO MGIEP.

2

The 51st Climb

**AN ATHLETE FULFILS THE LIFELONG
DREAM OF A STUDENT WITH DISABILITIES**

Greece

Waking up after a good night's sleep at the camp at 2400 m, Marios Giannakou secures Eleftheria Tosiou on to his back, ready to complete the last leg of the climb up to Mount Olympus.

A few hundred meters to the summit at Mount Mytikas, the highest peak of Mount Olympus, and a few more hours before the two of them look at Greece from up above.

For Giannakou, this is his 51st climb up the mountain. For Tosiou, it is a lifelong wish—an impossible feat made possible simply because of the athlete's kindness.

A few weeks prior to the climb, when Tosiou, a twenty-two-year-old student with disabilities, met Giannakou through a common friend and told him of her desire of scaling Mount Olympus, the long-distance runner immediately took to fulfilling it.

Twenty-nine-year-old Giannakou had previously trekked 168 miles across the Al Marmoom Desert; ran the 155-mile, five-day Coastal Challenge 2020 in the jungles of Costa Rica; bagged the first place in a 93-mile cross-country race in Antarctica; and hiked Mount Olympus fifty times.

But these international races, medals and distinctions mean little to him when compared to the goal of his 51st climb. There is nothing more real than Tosiou's dream.

Of course, there are different challenges to prepare for this time. Winter is only a few months away and, most crucially, he's never done mountain climbing carrying a person on his back before. In fact, nothing of this kind had ever been done before! He has to work fast before the onset of snow. Giannakou quickly gets together a team that would help him reach the peak. He has a specially modified backpack made to carry Tosiou with him.

The most difficult part, though, is the psychological one. 'A man lost his life there a day before,' recollects Giannakou.

Regarded in Greek mythology as the seat of the gods, scaling Mount Olympus—with its jagged peaks, steep inclines and slippery rocks—is not for the faint-hearted. And while carrying a person on your back, it is twice as difficult and twice as many lives to be responsible for!

'There was some fear because there were cliffs to my front and to my back, but there was not real fear that we couldn't make it,' shares Tosiou, who is a fan of extreme sports and has been wheelchair-bound all her life.

On 5 October 2020, 9.02 a.m., she realizes her dream of reaching the summit.

'I was happy, I was moved . . . In the end, it was most intense when we came down and realized what we had done,' Tosiou says in wonder.

The happiness is evident on the faces of both Giannakou and Tosiou as the two pose for photographs wearing triumphant smiles, the Greek flag in their hands and a victorious stance upon finishing their momentous journey.

'I have never done something more beautiful. I think it has completed me as a person,' concludes Giannakou. Knowing the man's long list of accomplishments, his thought reinforces the power that acts of kindness rewards above all other achievements.

3

Fixing Stereotypes

A BAND OF WOMEN REPAIRING CARS AND MINDSETS

Burkina Faso

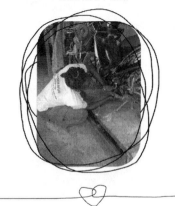

The constitution of Burkina Faso forbids gender discrimination, forced marriages and female circumcision, but the reality is far from this: 70 per cent of the girls in the country undergo genital mutilation. The myth that circumcised girls are healthier and women who are not circumcised cannot be faithful still prevails. The same is true for the countless women who are abused, oppressed and forced into marriage at an early age.

Take Joséphine Yameogo's case.

Born to a large family in a small village in the West African country, she was a month old when she was promised in marriage to a man over forty years her age. At seventeen, when she was set to marry her sixty-year-old future husband, Yameogo did the unthinkable and refused to go ahead with it. To add insult to injury, she married a man of her own choice. As could have been expected, she was disowned from the family and banished from the village.

But with three young children at home, Yameogo refused to let the limited resources and tremendous opposition stop her. Defying expectations was second nature to her. She trained in a profession traditionally reserved for men and went on to become the first woman in the country to work as a mechanic and open her own garage in the outskirts of the capital city of Ouagadougou. Soon, she was contributing to the family income, was being able to send her children to school and was also part of decision-making at home. She later found a job opportunity and is currently based in Turkey.

Today, Yameogo's success story is that of many others in Ouagadougou who are fighting entrenched traditions and gender stereotypes that confine women to house roles or low-paid unskilled labour, thanks to Center Féminin d'Initiation et d'Enseignement aux Métiers (CFIAM), a school that is training girls and women, often from disadvantaged backgrounds, in car mechanics, automotive electricity, electronics and body work.

'I realized that all of my older brothers who attended formal school faced unemployment at the end of their cycle. So, I decided to stop my studies in the fifth grade and move on to technical education,' says Mariam N'diaye Darankoum, who now runs her own electric workshop and also offers consulting services for purchasing electronic equipment.

The girls at CFIAM are met with kindness and understanding and are given psychological support and personal development courses. This helps them strengthen their self-esteem to overcome difficulties that they may face when seeking employment.

'Most of the girls who are attending this school come from very problematic families. They are completely in disarray and arrive in a state of emotional insecurity,' says Yvette, the course psychologist.

The school is a new start for these girls who learn that they can be masters of their lives, that they are really valuable.

In Burkina Faso, almost one in three children drop out before completing primary school. Secondary education is not an option for most young people, especially girls. And given the traditional education system's inability to translate to jobs, the popularity of CFIAM amongst young girls has grown tremendously.

The school in Ouagadougou, started in 2002, is the second of three branches in the country. It now has 200 students who study eight hours a day and six days a week with them.

In addition to mechanics and electronics, the girls are also taught entrepreneurship, management and development of business ideas to make sure that they are fully equipped to be independent, and in some cases even granted loans to start their own business.

'People don't believe it when I diagnose a problem with their car, dismissing it as "girl talk",' says Rookia, twenty-seven, who first attended car mechanic classes at the centre in 2016. 'But when it comes to men and marriage, if someone wants to love me, he must accept that I am an emancipated girl.'

4

A Bottle at a Time

**AN ECO-WARRIOR HELPS THE WATERWAYS
OF KERALA BREATHE PLASTIC-FREE**

India

Photograph by Pro Media

Every morning, long before dawn and long before the village of Manchadikkari wakes up, sixty-nine-year-old N.S. Rajappan tucks in his lungi and crawls down from his house to the Meenachil River. He slides on to a makeshift seat on a country boat, ready for the usual seventeen hours of collecting plastic waste from the waterways of Kerala's Vembanad Lake.

At a young age, Rajappan contracted poliomyelitis, which soon paralysed his legs. Work opportunities became sparse and he had to take up any small chore that came his way.

For more than half a decade, however, Rajappan has been doing a very important job—that of cleaning Vembanad Lake and other streams of Kumarakom in the Kottayam district.

'Somebody should remove the waste from the water. I am doing what is possible for me,' Rajappan says matter-of-factly. He has lived around these waters his entire life and knowing that he is helping the waters breathe better gives him great happiness and purpose.

A day's worth of collecting waste usually gets Rajappan four sacks full of plastic bottles and a meagre Rs 12 that he uses to buy kerosene oil.

'It used to be more before Covid-19. The lack of tourists has reduced the waste,' he says with a grin, despite his income having taken a hit.

But his day does not end with the task of collection. Rajappan cleans, dries and organizes the waste for the local agency that comes to pick it up once in a few months.

His meals are taken care of by his sister and some generous locals who call on him to collect their plastic waste and give him money.

Rajappan recollects the painful look he sees on the faces of people as they watch him crawl. 'They take pity on me,' he says. But the positive man Rajappan is, he does not feel sad about his condition. 'I have had this deformity since my childhood. What is the point of feeling bad about it?' He flashes his coy smile.

In the half a decade of working as Vembanad's environmental saviour, Rajappan has not missed a day's work—except once, during the floods, when the water destroyed his house and he had to take refuge in a boat.

'I lost all the garbage I had collected over the months and was very disappointed. But I started work again immediately once things improved,' says the high-spirited Rajappan.

And he plans to continue to work every day, spreading kindness to the natural world around him, one plastic bottle at a time.

The only wish Rajappan has had is one for a bigger boat of his own, so he could cover more area and collect more garbage. His wish recently came true when a photograph of him by Kottayam-based photographer, Nandu K.S., went viral, inviting recognition and gifts from around the globe, including Prime Minister Narendra Modi, the Taiwanese government and Supreme Master Ching Hai. Rajappan has since received awards, a cash prize, a motorized wheelchair and, most importantly, his very own motorboat!

'I want to have a roof over my head and live there happily until my death,' the humble Rajappan concludes. And the simplicity of thought of this environmental champion cannot be better summarized.

5

Education First

**ONE ZAMBIAN CHANGES THE FATE
OF MANY THROUGH EDUCATION**

Zambia

Photograph by Eliza Powell

Dialess was fourteen when she was married off to a man twice her age. Her mother, who lost her husband to AIDS and got infected with the virus herself, saw no other way to provide her daughter with food and shelter. Once married, Dialess's husband took her out of school, leaving her desolate with lost dreams.

Dialess's story is similar to that of several more child brides in rural Zambia. Many girls drop out or do not enrol in school due to high levels of poverty, HIV/AIDS, child marriage and school-related gender-based violence. According to Girls Not

Brides, a global partnership of more than 1500 civil society organizations from over 100 countries committed to ending child marriage, Zambia has one of the highest child marriage rates in the world.

Alice Saisha was on the brink of becoming just another statistic.

From the Samfya District in rural Zambia, Saisha, the youngest of ten siblings, helped her widowed mother run the house by working as a maid after school and selling cassava leaves. And yet, often they could afford only one meal a day. 'Sometimes just a glass of water would do,' recollects Saisha, as she pictures her mother sitting in their unfinished house, a placid expression now replacing her otherwise sunny smile.

At fourteen, unable to meet the expenses of school, Saisha almost dropped out, destined to become a child bride.

'My dreams of education were shattered,' she remembers.

It was then that her community stepped in. They inquired when she started missing school and initiated a scholarship for her through their partnership with the Campaign for Female Education (CAMFED).

'My mother was so happy [when the scholarship came through]!'

For the first time, Saisha's mother saw kindness around her. She saw that there were others who could help protect her daughter. Now Saisha had a place to stay at school, three meals a day and all fees paid for. Even her uniform, stationery and sanitary protection was taken care of.

Saisha was supported from the eighth grade till tertiary education, and she made the most of the opportunity that was given to her.

Today, she has a diploma in human resource management, a bachelor's degree in sociology and a master's degree in development studies. She plans to pursue a PhD next.

Saisha wants to continue studying and give back to the community that changed her life forever. To enable this, she runs a poultry farming business and has supported eleven orphans with their secondary education and provided shelter for two girls.

'I support girls from distinct backgrounds; two were abandoned, others were almost married and the rest had no support. The oldest is studying pharmacy and the youngest is now in her eleventh grade, she wants to be a nurse,' Saisha chirps.

As a CAMFED District Operations Secretariat and an active member of the CAMFED Alumnae Association in rural Zambia, Saisha has been trained to help rural women set up business. She also works with officials and schools in her home district to keep vulnerable girls in school.

Saisha advocates the importance of education, free sanitary protection, saving and investing and creating more job opportunities—all of it with the goal of promoting young women's independence and empowerment.

You can tell from the gleam in her eyes that nothing gives Saisha more joy than to contribute to society and experience the difference kindness can make.

'We are the role models now in our communities. Together we can change the status quo,' says the charismatic Saisha, who joins the many girls who've been advocates of change and progress in rural Zambia.

6
A Right to Education

AN INTERVIEW WITH
CYNTHIA SALAS LOPEZ

Mexico

Article 26 of the Universal Declaration of Human Rights states that everyone has the right to education. Education shall be free, at least in the elementary and fundamental stages. Elementary education shall be compulsory. Technical and professional education shall be made generally available and higher education shall be equally accessible to all on the basis of merit.

Contrary to this, statistics show that between 2006 and 2018, 53,53,711 children and adolescents dropped out from primary and secondary education in Mexico. Veracruz contribute a total of 1,47,648 to this number, making it the state that recorded the second highest number of education dropouts in the country.

Cynthia Salas Lopez, a secondary teacher with over ten years of experience, is working to fight these figures with her initiative to reform the law that guarantees the right to education.

Over the years of your teaching experience, you have taught in various parts of Veracruz where you mention observing great cultural, social and economic differences amongst the children.

There are differences that are obvious. In the hamlet of Sabaneta, where I first taught, most of the adult population speak the Popoluca language in addition to Spanish and wear traditional attire. And even though the young dispel traditional clothing and have little command over their native language, there continues to remain an archaic mindset where girls drop out after high school to marry or be relegated to household chores.

In Los Mangos, where I taught next, it is the reverse, even though both towns are within the same municipality. Women are encouraged by their families to go to school, both in town and outside of it.

My most recent school experience has been in the town of Camarón de Tejeda. While the population is more technologically advanced and up to date here, with young people having access to information, there is a considerable number of unwanted teen pregnancies.

From the very first year of working, when I was still training to be a teacher, we were told of the problem of dropouts, but it was only when I began working that I realized the seriousness of the matter.

And you see a common thread that ties school dropouts in all these varying demographics . . .

School dropout is a multifactorial problem; it does not occur because of a single situation . . . These vary depending on the cultural, social, family or economic context of each student. In the first school, it was because of the ingrained macho culture that forced most women to leave their studies as soon as they finished high school. In the second, the school dropout came mainly from men who dropped out at the end of secondary school or in the middle of their baccalaureate to go work in other states and support their families. And in the last, with the teenage pregnancies, girls would dropout and leave their homes to live with the baby's father, who was often a schoolmate who'd also drop out to support his new family. This is in addition to cases of dropouts due to simple rebellion to not wanting to study.

As teachers, we can't do much when a student leaves except call the parents to request that they send their children to school again. But in most cases, the call is ignored and the students do not return.

There are no strict measures taken against parents who stop sending their children to school. Students are unprotected by the state, even though education is actually a human right, protected by the country's constitution.

And all of this led you to reform this law so as to guarantee, in a real way, the right to education for the students.

The reformed law will set in place an action protocol for teachers, educational authorities, parents and students in cases of school dropouts. It will enable teachers to report the cases of school dropouts so that they are investigated and followed up with action, and parents to understand that there will be legal consequences for not sending their children to school.

The law is yet to be approved but while we wait for that to happen, we're trying to start a dialogue—with the children and their parents about the importance of education, family planning and the use of contraception, about the parents' obligation to send their child to school and, in case of children with low grades, about an action plan to help them improve and not dropout from fear of failing.

Most of the population in Mexico is poor, so receiving an education is an important step towards improving their living conditions.

With such challenging and diverse circumstances, and with this being such a global issue, how do you think we should all approach education and teaching?

With kindness. Teaching must be practised with kindness. We work with children who come from varied sociocultural backgrounds and are experiencing a variety of emotions at this stage of their life, so our work goes beyond just teaching subjects. We must give them the love that they may not receive at home, advice that they do not dare to ask their parents or even the hug that they have not received in days.

7

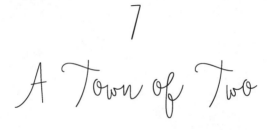

A Town of Two

TWO MEN FIGHT RADIATION
TO FEND FOR ANIMALS

Japan

When one of the biggest earthquakes ever recorded in history struck Japan, it triggered a tsunami that broke through the defences of the Fukushima nuclear plant, causing a radiation leak and a nuclear debacle considered to be one of the deadliest since the Chernobyl disaster in 1986. Living within 12.5 miles of the nuclear facility, 1,60,000 residents were asked to evacuate immediately. But only 1,59,998 heeded the warning.

Naoto Matsumura was one of the two.

From the small town of Tomioka, which is within Fukushima's 12.5-mile exclusion zone, Matsumura, too, fled at first. But with relatives turning him away for fear of contamination and evacuee camps cramped for space and short on resources, he returned home just as quickly.

'It was so silent in town that the only thing you could hear was the buzzing of the flies,' Matsumura says. 'It was crazy at first.' With no people or cars, empty buildings and no light or sound, Tomioka felt like a ghost town.

But Matsumura soon found company in the animals that had been left behind in the rush of escape.

His new family was him and his dogs, who were still at home when he returned. But as soon as he started feeding the dogs, he heard the cries of the ones in the neighbourhood. Several people had thought that they would come back in a few days and hadn't taken their pets along with them when they evacuated. When Matsumura went to check on them, he found them all tied up and hungry.

Matsumura realized that all of them needed his help. 'They'd all gather around barking up a storm as soon as they heard my truck. Like, "we're thirsty" or "we don't have any food." So, I just kept making the rounds.' He began feeding them too.

Soon, he also took pigs, ponies, ostriches and cows under his care.

But despite his best efforts, a lot of cattle perished, not only due to starvation but also due to the government's decision to euthanize them under the belief that livestock couldn't be cared for or consumed after the evacuation.

'Now it's all bones; it's easier to look at, but back then, it was really gruesome,' Matsumura recalls of a barn near his home. 'There were flies and maggots on the corpses.'

This angered Matsumura.

For the kind man, all lives must be treated fairly, and to kill one without reason is out of question.

Today, Matsumura lives a life dedicated to protecting the animals left behind from the tragedy and they all survive on help from the outside.

'At first I was scared of getting cancer or leukaemia, but I refuse to worry about it any more,' says Matsumura, nonchalantly taking a drag from the cigarette that he loves so much. When asked about it, he jokes about how quitting it might get him ill now.

On the advice of doctors, Matsumura eats relief food delivered from the outside and drinks spring water that has been checked for contamination. He has no electricity and no running water. He does have solar panels that he uses to power his computer and cell phone.

He is accompanied by Sakae Kato, the second of the two men living in Fukushima's exclusion zone, who takes care of forty-one cats. He had sixty-four to begin with, and a dog named Pochi. Both men know that they are shouldering a risk that no other has taken on, but they refuse to leave the animals they care about behind.

Tests show that Matsumura has been exposed to radiation that is seventeen times more than any normal person, which is not surprising since he was eating contaminated food when he returned.

'They told me that I wouldn't get sick for thirty or forty years. I'll most likely be dead by then anyway, so I couldn't care less,' says the sixty-two-year-old Matsumura laughingly, who has happily accepted the title of the guardian of Fukushima's animals.

MAKE
KINDNESS
CONTAGIOUS

THE BOOK OF INSTRUCTIONS

Rohini Kejriwal
(India)

In the dead of night,
she opened the book of instructions
to dissolve the pain,
the unbearableness of loss
raw wounds and heartburn

1.
Heal the world
by starting with yourself
no more fight or flight
take it one day at a time.

2.
Strive for discipline,
another form of self love
do not underestimate
the joy of monotony.

3.
Don't let the burden
of worry or perfection
weigh you down
embrace the in-betweenness.

4.
Water will save you
drink plenty,
dip your feet in,
float, don't sink.

5.
Open your eyes,
let the mysteries in
don't lose sight of
the road not taken.

* Curated by *The Alipore Post*

8

A SYRIAN PARTNERING WITH BEES TO HELP IMPROVE FELLOW REFUGEES' MENTAL HEALTH

Syria/United Kingdom

Ali Alzein applied for asylum in the UK in January 2014.

A Syrian born and raised in Damascus, Alzein lived in the city with his parents who ran a knitwear business with a few stores in Syria and one in London. He graduated with a degree in fashion design to help with the business. 'We had a nice, normal life,' recollects Alzein.

This was before the Syrian revolution in 2011. As the protests against the government strengthened, the army besieged cities and obstructed food and medicine supplies to the citizens.

Alzein and his family mounted support and provided for those living in areas blocked by the army for a year, until the government found them out. The family's factory and home were burnt down and their locality was declared a conflict zone, forcing them to leave Syria immediately.

Alzein had a job offer in Egypt and left for it the very next day. He stayed in the job for about a year, until the Egypt government started arresting Syrians who were wanted by the Syrian government and sent them back.

Alzein was arrested, but luckily was granted asylum in the UK, where he dived head first into the luxury fashion industry, with a job at Harrods. However, having grown up in an environment that instilled kindness, he continued to volunteer by servicing customers in the day and working at refugee camps whenever he had a minute to spare.

The shock of the two divergent worlds drastically affected his mental health. He left his job tearful every day. With the refugee camps he was working in and the background of everything that had happened and was still happening back home, the customers at Harrods looked like they came from a different planet! 'I was really suffering from PTSD and severe depression,' admits Alzein. He began to feel disassociated from the people he met at work and in February 2020, he quit his job.

In the time that he spent at home healing, he realized that working in the garden was helping him a lot. He got a beehive for his garden, having learnt beekeeping from his grandfather as a kid at the farm back home. But he soon found that the bees did more than just provide him with honey.

'Being around bees is really therapeutic. It calms a person down,' he says, even as a plume of black bees buzz around his face.

Alzein knew that there are refugees like him who lived with PTSD and depression from traumatic experiences that they carried within themselves.

With the therapeutic and environmental benefits of beekeeping in mind, he founded Bees and Refugees to not only build a network of trained refugees who could use beekeeping as therapy or a source of income, but also help grow the black bee population that was thought to be extinct.

'Bees work together, they strive for unity,' shares Alzein. With his own initiative, he seeks to apply this principle to provide a safe space for everyone to heal and grow as a community together.

Free workshops for refugees was only the beginning. He then aimed to crowdfund £38,000 to place fifty beehives across London to make them easily accessible for all refugees who wanted to learn beekeeping. While the global pandemic that began in 2020 has made it harder to raise funds for the refugee crisis that is still raging, Alzein continues to find solutions like taking workshops in schools in exchange for them hosting the beehives.

The goal for the project is to set up beehives directly in the refugee camps, where he believes people need it the most, over the next two years.

'I felt that both bees and refugees are under attack and that they could work together to support each other,' says Alzein, summarizing his vision, his smile not fading for a minute throughout.

9
Programming Success

**AN INITIATIVE TO HELP
GIRLS FIND SUCCESS**

Armenia

Shogher Mikayelyan was in a local orphanage in her hometown of Gyumri, Armenia, leading a tour group of American volunteers, when one of the girls living there thanked them for visiting but also added that she knew that they would all forget the children as soon as they left.

Taken aback by the brutal honesty, Mikayelyan promised her that she would come back, but the little girl would not believe it. 'Don't promise something that you won't be able to keep. Anyone who needs us comes here but as soon as they leave, they will always forget us and will never come back,' Mikayelyan recalls her saying.

The girl's words stayed with Mikayelyan. She wanted to keep her promise, but she also wanted to do something more that would help them tap into their potential and become self-sufficient. And when Ara and Richard Chackerian, two American-Armenians who'd been a part of that volunteer group she'd led, mirrored her dream, she immediately began researching mentorship programmes for the girls.

There were none that she found in Gyumri. And so, the three decided to develop one to solve the lack of educational resources and accessibility.

Founded in 2009, Nor Luyce, meaning 'new light', enables teenage girls from orphanages, vulnerable families and low-income families to achieve financial independence through one-on-one mentorship, skill building and higher education with a focus on career planning and communication skills.

The programme is built around three phases that lasts one year each. In the initial phase, mentees form a support group and network with mentors through one-on-one and group meetings. This helps the girls identify with role models and also form close bonds with other mentees who motivate each other through the next two years.

During the summer, when the girls are on a school break, the programme also offers English and computer classes.

In the second phase, the girls develop life and leadership skills and learn career planning through tests and professional interactions.

The third phase is for mentees to pick up job skills, take a step towards university education and qualify for Nor Luyce scholarships that provide for their higher education.

'The girls, especially ones from the orphanage, would marry anyone because they saw him as a way out of the orphanage,' says Mikayelyan. 'Many were subjected to domestic violence and conditioned to believe that it is their fault.'

With Nor Luyce, Mikayelyan wants these girls to understand that there are other ways to get out of the orphanage—by having a career and asserting their independence. She wants them to recognize the power they have to stand up for themselves and break out of their shell.

'Thanks to the mentors, I have become more industrious, optimistic and learnt much about self-development,' says Silva, a mentee.

In the eleven years since its inception, the programme has empowered 191 girls, sixty-six out of whom came from one-parent households, nineteen from no-parent households and 106 from two-parent households with low socio-economic status—all of whom are currently employed and have conducted nearly 7000 hours of meetings in subjects such as overcoming fears, work ethic, interpersonal skills and leadership training. Nor Luyce has also been granted the United Nations Economic and Social Council (ECOSOC) accreditation from the UN.

With the accreditation, Nor Luyce is applying for a variety of grants and projects that will help to develop the organization. Their aim is to grow the mentee numbers and provide a bigger space for the girls to feel safe, learn and grow.

'I found my luyce [light] in the small and beautiful family [of Nor Luyce] with big love and warmth,' says Ani, another mentee. And the love, support and kindness that Mikayelyan has worked to create through Nor Luyce cannot be summed up more perfectly.

10

One with the River

**A WOMAN'S FIGHT TO PROTECT
THE WATERS IN HER VILLAGE**

Bosnia and Herzegovina

It was mid-December 2018. Maida Bilal was in Sarajevo for a meeting when she got a call from a friend standing on the small wooden bridge that had only been recently renamed the 'Bridge of the Brave Women of Kruščica'. The friend was crying as she shared the good news with Bilal—the regional court of Bosnia and Herzegovina had just cancelled all environmental and construction permits for the dams on the Kruščica River.

Bilal recalls crying and laughing all at once when she heard the news, jumping in the streets, skipping the meeting and running to find a bus back home to her village, Kruščica.

They had just won a 503 day-long battle.

It began in early July 2017 when Bilal learnt that heavy machines were en route Kruščica to begin work on the dams on the Kruščica River. To get to the site of construction, the bulldozers had to cross the very wooden bridge that her friend would later call her from, which connected their village to the forest and the river. It was here that Bilal and 300 other villagers stood in an impromptu peaceful protest, blocking the path of the bulldozers twenty-four hours a day in eight-hour shifts each.

Anticipating that violence would be guaranteed if only men were involved, the women took the front seat at the protests, not knowing that their physical safety was on the line.

Less than two months into their barricade of the bridge, at the dawn of 24 August 2017, a special police unit in full riot gear attacked the women to clear the bridge. Bilal was hit in the head and her father was beaten as well when he came forward to protect her. He was among the twenty-three arrested that day, although the charges against them were dropped later.

With the protestors violently removed, construction crew moved in to start work on the two power plants, which would have provided only about 1.1 MW of energy combined, but the villagers continued their protest, this time putting their bodies between a backhoe and the construction site. Finally, the crew left and the bridge protest resumed.

The Balkans, where Bosnia and Herzegovina is located, is home to the last free-flowing rivers in Europe. But the region has seen a massive hydropower boom, with 436 mini hydropower projects built, planned or underway across Bosnia and Herzegovina alone, and thousands more in other parts of the Balkans, which have risked sixty-nine endemic fish species and 40 per cent of Europe's endangered freshwater mollusc species. Notably, 95 per cent of the power generated in Bosnia and Herzegovina through such projects is exported to Western Europe, with no benefit to the locals who suffer through the destruction and displacement.

For over 1,50,000 locals like Bilal, the river not only provides drinking water but is also home to memories of growing up. It is a part of them. And having witnessed nature around them being destroyed for years, the fight for protecting their land and nature and showing it kindness was spontaneous and rapid. Add to that the anger that had been growing since 2016, when the municipal government first approved the hydropower plants without consultation of the local communities.

After the police attack, Bilal channelled her determination further to co-found the Eko Bistro Citizens' Association and fight the construction of the dams on several other fronts—by organizing community protests in the region's capital, leveraging media attention and working with a lawyer to challenge the legality of the construction permits.

In 2018, the local court began annulling the environmental and other permits for the dam construction in response to the protests. However, lacking faith in the judicial system, the women continued to protest.

It was only when the court cancelled all permits for the dams did the women let up—on 19 December 2018.

But Bilal, who is happy to have put a hold on the dams, believes that this is just one battle in an ongoing war. She is grateful for the increasing encouragement and support, and is counting on it as the court battles begin. It is what gives her hope and she is certain that they will save the rivers.

For her continued effort in protecting the Kruščica River, Maida Bilal was awarded the Goldman Environmental Prize 2021.

11

Advocating for Justice

For her thirteenth birthday, Dipika Badal's father took her to an HIV orphanage near their home. The plan was to celebrate with the children at the orphanage by distributing chocolates and playing games. But while she was ecstatic and so were the others, she noticed a little girl who wasn't taking part in the celebrations. When she asked her why, the girl said that she hated birthdays because while others celebrated, she counted her days on Earth and 'lived by the calendar'.

Badal was overwhelmed by her words.

Once home, she relayed this conversation, which made her both sad and angry, to her parents who told her: 'The world does not provide justice to all, and not everyone is happy.'

Badal knew immediately that she was not okay with that. She wanted to work for the justice of everyone and towards bringing happiness to others, changing their everyday with kindness.

When she came across the youth-led NGO 'We' for Change a year later, it was an instant connect. 'I loved their vision and what they were doing.'

Badal has been working with the NGO since 2014 and was made president of the organization in 2019, a post she held on to until March 2021. Over the years, she has implemented over ten projects and more than thirty programmes, reaching more than 5000 youths in her home country, Nepal.

'"We" for Change currently work in five areas—environment sustainability, health, disaster preparedness, youth civic engagement and youth leadership—and all projects under them,' says Badal.

Working towards HIV protection and healthcare, in 2018, the team modified a van to travel to the most vulnerable regions in Nepal that did not have equal access to healthcare to provide HIV testing. And amongst the many interactive ways that the organization has raised awareness towards HIV susceptibility such as dance, sports, yoga and meditation, the team took to social media with an innovative music video on the importance of condoms for HIV prevention.

'The condom song! This was a lot of fun to make. We had a *dohori* (singing) session about the importance of condoms and HIV/AIDS, and we assimilated it to make the video,' says Badal, breaking into a verse of the positively infectious tune that advocated for people to stop being shy about condoms.

They have also used a van to build a mobile library to reach the children in the most affected districts after the 2015 Nepal earthquake. But Badal's favourite project has been the more recently launched Pahal: Justice for Green Generation, for which she organized silent, peaceful protests with 150 students and over 1000 local commuters.

'I love this quote by Malala Yousafzai that says: "When the whole world is silent, even one voice is powerful". I saw the whole world be silent about the pollution problem in Kathmandu that was causing chronic diseases in the citizens, and so I, along with one of my closest friends, decided to protest,' says Badal.

'At the time, many other groups were also conducting campaigns against air pollution alongside us, and the protests caught the attention of the Ministry of Environment who installed pollution metres and dustbins and worked to systematize traffic and electric vehicles.' It isn't enough, Badal says, but it's a step in the right direction.

Currently, Badal has completed her BSc in Forestry, and continues to plan and implement long-term strategies, and work towards raising awareness on climate action, environment sustainability and youth empowerment through different networks that she is involved in, namely: 'We' for Change, Global Changemakers, Diana Awards and One Young World. 'We have to continue to teach more people to respect life and bring happiness to more people around us and, most importantly, we have to make people believe that they must trust young people and invest in young people,' she concludes with a smile.

* This story was adapted from an article originally published on Faze Media, a kindness collaborator of UNESCO MGIEP.

12
No Language Barrier

**BRIDGING THE GAP BETWEEN REFUGEES
AND LOCALS WITH LANGUAGE**

Switzerland

Out of the taxi window, Lisa Sophia Marti can see her destination approach. 'Please, brother, can you stop here for me?' she says in the Moroccan dialect, and the driver's face twists into one of pleasant astonishment. For someone like her to be speaking his tongue!

While pursuing her bachelor's degree in social science at the University of Bern, Switzerland, Lisa travelled to Morocco to study Arabic. Her passion for political and Middle Eastern studies brought her to the country to learn its language and work with a local NGO that supports refugees. But her newly acquired language skills were of no use on the streets, because the standard Arabic that she was learning was nothing like the spoken dialect.

'It was very frustrating,' Lisa recollects.

Luckily for Lisa, she got by due to the kindness of strangers who helped her learn bits of the local dialect. Like her fellow passengers in the shared taxi, who taught her what to say when she wanted the driver to stop the car. Or the old man who went through the local names of each vegetable she bought from him, just so she could learn them all. Or some other acquaintances who taught her the local way to say, 'I'm really great.'

Being able to converse with locals in their tongue changed their interactions with her. 'I was amazed to see how something so simple could open so many doors and make me feel much more integrated into daily life.'

Lisa became aware of a similar language barrier between locals and refugees back home too. In the German part of Switzerland, people learn standard German, but locals speak a very distinct dialect. Knowing first-hand that language is the first step to feeling part of the society that you are living in, she immediately got together with a few friends to find a solution.

They wanted to break this barrier between refugees and locals and, more importantly, give the refugees a choice between what they wanted to learn, what was important to learn and what was available to learn, all with the ultimate aim to create a more inclusive society.

Their project, 'voCHabular', does just that through a self-study tool in the form of a book and an app that helps facilitate interaction and thereby the entry of refugees into everyday life in the country.

The first batch of 2000 copies sold out in the first month, and the project now includes interactive books covering Arabic, Farsi and English translations to (Swiss) German.

But a by-product of the project that Lisa cherishes equally is the community that they have built. She was certain that she wanted refugee voices to be part of the project and so, she brought together a team of over sixty volunteers, both refugees and locals, to co-create the first book.

Owing to the pandemic, voCHabular has had to adapt to an innovative online-offline hybrid model, which has slowed down work, but the team perseveres in any way they can. Like partnering with 'Food for All', a food bank system started by their co-president—an undocumented refugee himself—to donate 300 books along with food for all those who have had their German classes put on hold. They also created a solidarity fund for voCHabular members that struggled during these challenging times and participated in online campaigns to raise awareness about the refugees in Switzerland and at the borders of Europe. All of this happening while they continued to translate the book in new languages like French, Turkish, Tigrinya and Spanish.

In December 2020, voCHabular celebrated their fifth anniversary. 'We tend to focus on offering rational solutions to global challenges and we forget about the feelings. A big part of being human is our relations with one another,' says Lisa, who believes that kindness, as strangers had shown her in Morocco, is what builds trust and connections.

13

Bibliomotocarro

**A RETIRED TEACHER'S JOURNEY
TO GET BOOKS TO EVERY CHILD**

Italy

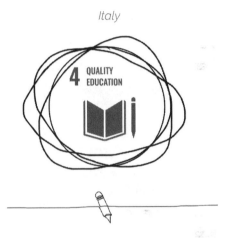

There's a gush of warm breeze as the aqua blue van chugs to a stop along the stoned pathways of the village in Italy with 270 inhabitants, an organ sounding its arrival and calling a young boy and girl out of their home. The siblings run to it, thrilled, while a few grown-ups stand to watch.

Antonio La Cava, a childish grin on his face, is on his weekly rounds through the isolated villages of Basilicata and has stopped in San Paolo Albanese, 100 kilometres away from his own village of Ferrandina. He wants to make sure that the two children who live in this village get their fill of books from his travelling library.

Bibliomotocarro, as La Cava named it, is a library of wheels that the retired elementary teacher has been running for almost twenty years now.

Having forty-two years of teaching experience behind him, La Cava was worried about growing old in a country of non-readers! Upon being encouraged by his students to do something about it, he immediately got to searching for a solution.

There was a growing disaffection with books and La Cava believed it was essential to find or maybe even create new readers. He began to look for them in the small villages with 1000 inhabitants or less in the south of Italy, where children had a lack of access to them. La Cava's motto is simple: no child must be denied the right to have a book that they desire, directly in their hand. And his 'Ape' three-wheeler van, appropriately modified to have a red-tiled roof, smoking chimney, built-in shelves and walk-in library, is just the humble vehicle for the endeavour.

Mobile libraries have a long history of bringing the knowledge of books to remote villages. The only difference being that instead of vans like La Cava's bookmobile, they were mostly horse-drawn wagons. But with the emergence of public libraries in towns, bookmobiles gradually ceased to be and readers in smaller villages were forgotten. La Cava wants Bibliomotocarro to be accessible, just as culture should be. He hopes to change the understanding of books as an expression of aristocratic culture, by a few and for a few, to an expression of the masses.

La Cava currently has an inventory of 1000 books, a lot of them donated by people from the towns he visits, with which he travels over 500 kilometres through the villages of Basilicata, all on his own money. His website lists a schedule of weekly stops and the cheerful man is always greeted by a rush of equally happy kids eager to start their next book, without a loan register to sign because the kind La Cava believes in harvesting trust.

La Cava believes that books and the written word are essential, and children without them are often left alone. Over the years, La Cava has extended his 'The Books on Wheels' service to include an initiative called 'White Book'. Kids from one village are invited to write the first chapter of a story in a plain exercise book he brings with him, which is then carried to the next town where another group of readers write the next chapter and so on. A travelling writing workshop, La Cava calls it.

14

Healing Together

**A PROGRAMME THAT BRINGS YOUNG
REFUGEES TO COPE WITH LIFE IN EXILE**

Bangladesh

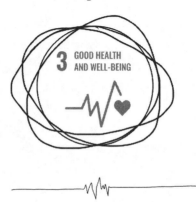

Somewhere amidst the labyrinth of tinned roofs and tarpaulin, on the dusty yellow grounds, a group of fourteen children are knelt down in a huddle. All eyes are on thirteen-year-old Myshara, who is inquiring with the others about how they are feeling and leading the group to discuss ways of coping with the trauma of living a life away from home, as a refugee in the Kutupalong camp—the largest of thirty-four camps in Bangladesh's Cox's Bazar district.

Currently, there are more than eighty-two million refugees in the world who have fled violence, human rights violations and persecution—the highest recorded in recent history. Myanmar is one of the top five countries contributing to this number. Of the almost one million Rohingya people who have fled Myanmar, Cox's Bazar houses 9,00,000.

Myshara is one of them.

Those displaced wish to return home, but until it is safe to do so, they are forced to build a life of dignity and hope in the camps, which also entails coping with the trauma of loss and suffering. A life in exile takes a mighty toll on one's mental well-being and the peer-to-peer mental health programme for young refugees run by UNHCR, the UN Refugee Agency, with three partner organizations—Relief International, Food for the Hungry and GK—aims to make coping with this trauma easier. Their vision is to help transcend the culture of silence that surrounds mental health in the Rohingya community and initiate conversations about feelings in the 10–18 age group.

The programme began in 2019 with a small group of children, which has now grown to almost 30,000 children. The key to their successful growth? A project that is helmed by peer leaders their own age, who have been identified and trained by the Rohingya community psychosocial volunteers.

But the programme is also designed to build each child's leadership skills and self-confidence.

And the proof of its success is seen in leaders like Myshara, and eleven-year-old Hamida, who now talks confidently about how the programme helped her overcome her fears and how her group leads discussions on mental peace and practises breathing exercises when they are feeling anxious.

Several young leaders say that the role was daunting in the beginning, but each one of them has embraced the responsibility and met with their group regularly to help each other.

For many who lost friends and loved ones when fleeing from Myanmar in 2017, the programme has also taught them resilience, observes Mahmudul Alam, an assistant mental health and psychosocial support officer with UNHCR.

Some of the leaders have gone on to integrate family and neighbours during the pandemic, which restricted their own peer group meetings. Like eighteen-year-old Muhammad, who, when unable to meet his group due to the Covid-19 restrictions, spoke to people around him to encourage them to talk about their feelings and also comfort them.

The group meetings resumed in June 2021, this time with smaller numbers to keep in mind social distancing norms, but the programme has equipped the children with skills that they will use to help themselves, their families and the community for life.

15

Fashion Moguls in the Making

AN AFRICAN ENTREPRENEUR WORKING TO SKILL FASHION-PRENEURS

Nigeria

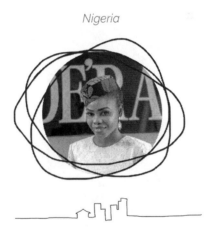

'It might sound like a cliché, but I want to be the change I wish to see in the world. I understand that change begins with me, hence my relentless efforts to keep it up,' smiles Aminat Aderayo Animashaun, a bright *dhuku* neatly tied on her head to match her long ankara earrings.

The thirty-four-year-old Nigerian is the CEO of Switt Fashion and Leather Works, which produces handmade shoes, bags and accessories made from leather and fabrics such as ankara, *aso-ofi*, *adire*, silk and satin. The company, based in Ibadan, was founded with the aim to see good quality, locally produced products make its way around the globe while simultaneously supporting job creation in Nigeria.

According to the federal bureau of statistics, the rate of unemployment in Nigeria was 18.8 per cent in 2017 and 23.13 per cent by the final quarter of 2018, and this was what Aderayo wanted to correct. But to achieve her goal, she first had to set an example of the job possibilities at home. And so, she founded De'rayo Vocational Limited in 2018, an initiative to empower women and youth through skill acquisition—like shoemaking, bead making, accessory making, textile design and photography—so they can change their job-seeking orientation to that of job creation and entrepreneurship.

'It is really upsetting to see that the youth isn't encouraged or supported by the government with infrastructures and policies to make sure they thrive,' says Aderayo. 'What is Nigeria's future when the leaders of tomorrow are not prepared for the future?'

Aderayo, herself, has a diploma in marketing from Olabisi Onabanjo University, a DELF certificate in French and has a B.Sc. in entrepreneurial and business administration from the Nigeria National Open University. She has also studied entrepreneurial management at the Enterprise Development Centre, Lagos Business School, under the World Bank's WomenX scholarship.

Aderayo had been interested in fashion as early as the age of six when she recalls stitching fabrics together. By the time she was a teenager, she told her mother that she wanted to learn fashion designing and so, she started to train at her friend's shop after school.

Her own journey to become a fashion designer taught her that a future and career did not have to be degree-driven but instead skill-based. She realized that it could not be left up to the government to help provide such education.

'There's a common misconception that kindness has to do with giving money or material things. But kindness comes in many forms, including volunteering, teaching and mentoring,' says Aderayo, who believes that the youth she trains can be carriers of kindness and can pay it forward with the skills they learn.

In the three years since its conception, De'rayo Vocational Limited has trained 6800 young people, and Aderayo is now working to reach 10,000. She does all this with her personal funds, although collaborations with like-minded entrepreneurs and NGOs have helped train women and youth in various other skills.

'You've got to get out there and make it happen for yourself,' says Aderayo. 'Don't just sit there and wait for people to give you that golden dream.'

In the coming years, Aderayo hopes to turn De'rayo Vocational Limited into a conventional university so that they can produce more indigenous fashion-preneurs, and she's not resting until then.

16

Musical Refuge

WHEN VENEZUELAN REFUGEES FOUND SOLIDARITY THROUGH MUSIC

Chile

Thirty-five-year-old Ana Marvez considered herself rather lucky for securing a minimum wage job as a secretary in an art school in Chile.

Not only had she found work within a few weeks of coming to the Chilean capital of Santiago, but she also managed to stay connected to her former career as a music teacher and choir leader back home in Venezuela.

Of the over 4,57,000 Venezuelan refugees and migrants now living in Chile, very few have had similar good fortune. A majority of them are forced to take on any job they can find to afford basic amenities. The same is true for professional musicians that are part of this number—most working as cashiers, nannies, security guards, doormen or any other work that helps them get by.

It wasn't a surprise then that shortly after joining the school, Marvez started receiving heaps of CVs from displaced Venezuelan musicians desperately seeking work.

Marvez was aware that a lack of practice would lead to a loss of skill and the many years of training. Knowing the quality of musicians that Venezuela—one of the world's most prestigious music programmes and network of youth orchestras—produces, Marvez just could not let that happen.

On a whim, she took part of the pile of CVs home and started calling the applicants to ask if they were interested in starting an orchestra or taking music classes over the weekends. Almost all agreed immediately. In fact, many even got their friends on board for the project.

And so, Marvez started the Fundación Música para la Integración (Music for Integration Foundation).

With a whopping 350 members to date, the project includes a symphony orchestra, a choral ensemble and several music classes for children. A majority of the members are volunteers, who are simply happy to have got the opportunity to play music, although the foundation does equally share the earnings received from the classes and the concerts they perform across Chile.

But the foundation means more than supplementary income for most of them. It aims to integrate immigrants through their talent and professions and provide the impulse of the social and cultural development of Chile by playing top music and teaching the new generations of musicians. 'The foundation has become something of a space for emotional rehabilitation as they go through the process of adapting to life in Chile,' Marvez says. It is a home away from home and an antidote to their loneliness and depression.

With the pandemic, the foundation and its members have had to adapt yet again. The concerts cancelled and no possibility for in-person rehearsals, they have had to limit practice and music classes and shift both online. For the income that music brought them, fundraisers are being held to help buy food and send money back to their families in Venezuela.

There is no saying when the foundation will resume concerts and other offline activity, but Marvez and the organization's all-female board of directors have big plans. The next goal is to reach out to other vulnerable populations, including the LGBTI community and people with disabilities.

For now, though, Marvez is proud of the collective strength that the foundation has brought to displaced people, especially women like her.

'We have shown the world that a woman who has every disadvantage because of being a foreigner was able to bring such a beautiful project to fruition,' Marvez concludes.

17

We Need to Talk

**AN INTERVIEW WITH
İLAYDA ESKITAŞÇIOĞLU**

Turkey

İlayda Eskitaşçioğlu is a human rights lawyer and the founder of We Need to Talk, an NGO that aims to fight period poverty and menstruation stigma in Turkey and the Middle East by providing menstrual products to women and girls from vulnerable communities and by starting honest and open conversations about menstruation.

How was We Need to Talk born?

Unfortunately, out of a disaster. In the 2011 earthquake in Van, Turkey, my family worked to send rescue packages to those affected and I realized that we hadn't included menstrual products. That's when it struck me—menstruation doesn't stop for disasters! And we, coming from privilege and so used to having silent conversations about menstruation, are unaware of the others who don't have the means for menstrual products. It was then that the seed was sowed.

It germinated in 2013 when 'menstruating women' were added to the definition of the word 'dirty' in the Turkish Language Association dictionary.

But it was in 2016, when my study in human rights took me to the other corner of the world, to Beijing for the G(irls)20 Summit, to really start my feminist journey. It was there that I felt the need to do something to address the period poverty and period taboo in my country, and I began immediately once I got back. Of course, this was the time of the coup attempt in Turkey and if it was hard earlier, it had become impossible now.

Tell us about your first project.

After innumerable unanswered emails to politicians, NGOs, famous feminists, I decided to start on my own—with a bake sale and a lemonade booth at my high school. With the money that was raised, I organized our first field project in an economically disadvantaged neighbourhood in Ankara with doctors and high school volunteers.

And you've reached over 30,000 more people since.

And so many more to come! Most importantly, after my first field project, my co-manager and business partner Bahar Aldanmaz joined me, and we are continuing our first field project together. We have distributed menstrual products, conducted training on making their own sustainable sanitary pads, had workshops to help the girls track their menstrual cycles and listen to their bodies and, most importantly, had open conversations with the girls and boys (on the occasions that we do have them be part of the workshops) about menstruation to help get rid of the stigma associated with it.

Now, we are working to grow our reach across the Middle East with our sanitary materials distribution, trainings, workshops and interactive sessions. To break period stigma, public conversations are extremely important. But to really make a dent in period poverty, I believe the solution is fair taxation. As of now, menstruators pay 18 per cent value added tax on something as essential as sanitary wear when they are bleeding every month. And for many, it makes these products inaccessible. Which is why we are working to put together petitions and have recently managed to get a member of parliament to submit a legislation proposal to decrease taxation and to provide free sanitary materials as part of the universal healthcare system in Turkey. We are unsure of the success of it as of now, but I still see it as a success.

You talk about kindness being integral to these conversations . . .

Absolutely. We have to be empathetic to the background that the seasonal agricultural workers, Syrian refugees and pre-teen girls we interact with come from. They all take time to open up and share their stories, often coming from vulnerable conditions, having gone through traumatic experiences and conditioned to believe in period stigma.

In Turkey and part of the Middle East, there is this strange tradition of slapping a child when they first have their period. Some people say it is to remind them of their womanhood and to protect their honour, some say it is in order to make their cheeks pink. But you can imagine what that might be like for a young girl who is going through something as scary and confusing as bleeding.

You also have to be sensitive to the other cultural nuances, for example, tampons or menstrual cups are not easily accepted because of the importance of virginity in the community and the understanding that these products may cause women to lose theirs.

Kindness becomes integral to create a safe space to have all these honest conversations.

'In Turkey, to have raised menstruation as part of public and political conversation is really something. Of course, there is so much more to do, but we are happy about the progress and happy and motivated,' says the positive Eskitaşçioğlu. She is currently a PhD student studying international human rights law at Koç University in Istanbul, Turkey; one of the seventeen Young Leaders for the SDGs endorsed by United Nations; a fellow at the UNESCO Chair for Gender Equality and Sustainable Development; a G(irls)20 ambassador; a Stanford AMENDS Fellow; and a researcher at the Center for Gender Studies (KOÇ-KAM). She is also working on a children's book with her business partner Bahar on menstruation to explore more ways to expand their reach.

THE RAGGED AND THE BEAUTIFUL

Safiya Sinclair
(Jamaica)

Doubt is a storming bull, crashing through
the blue-wide windows of myself. Here in the heart
of my heart where it never stops raining,

I am an outsider looking in. But in the garden
of my good days, no body is wrong. Here every
flower grows ragged and sideways and always

beautiful. We bloom with the outcasts,
our soon-to-be sunlit, we dreamers. We are strange
and unbelonging. Yes. We are just enough

of ourselves to catch the wind in our feathers,
and fly so perfectly away.

* Curated by *The Alipore Post*

18

A Resting Place

A WOMAN'S DETERMINATION TO ENSURE
EVERY REFUGEE A DECENT BURIAL

Venezuela

'Don't you know me? I'm the crazy one that buries the dead,' Sonia Bermúdez says with a laugh as two police officers carrying out a routine check in the border region of La Guajira, Colombia stop her.

Sixty-five-year-old Bermúdez is on her way to build graves alone, unlike other times when she travels with a coffin in the back of her truck, the family of the deceased squeezed around it and the medical release papers within reach on the dashboard, to bury the dead.

In 1996, when authorities informed her that there wasn't any place left to bury unclaimed and unidentified victims of Colombia's fifty-year-long armed conflict and drug-related violence, she refused to take it sitting down. She invaded a 5.5-hectare plot of land that belonged to the district of Riohacha. There, she set up a cemetery, Gente Como Uno (People like Us).

With the increasing economic and political crisis in neighbouring Venezuela, Bermúdez's focus has shifted to refugees and migrants who ran away from home in hope for food and safety but did not survive. It began with her helping one family bury their loved one in the charity's cemetery. Now, she is the only one to call when there is a death in the Venezuelan community in La Guajira.

To date, more than 300 displaced Venezuelans are buried in her cemetery.

The municipal cemetery charges a fee of at least $100 for burial spaces. Coffins start at $200. For migrants who make about $5 a day, these amounts are beyond unaffordable.

A coroner with forty-six years of practice at a medical examiner's office in Riohacha, Bermúdez could not stand the differential treatment that such families received. Her non-profit organization works to eliminate this disparity and make sure that the poor and vulnerable get a dignified burial, regardless of their nationality or the family's ability to pay. So attached she is to her purpose that she calls them *mis muertos* or 'my dead'.

On most days, she is in the cemetery building tombs, unbothered by the relentless sun that burns down on the dry orange ground and no company except the one workman, the occasional cars and many crickets. On other days she's busy making sure that the families that have lost their loved ones are met with kindness.

When she receives a call from the hospital or a migrant family, she collects the corpse, brings it to the cemetery where the family prays an 'Our Father' or an 'Ave Maria' and sprinkles holy water, which has been sourced from a local priest, on the coffin.

'The hardest moment is when I finish closing off the tomb,' she says. Every tomb is plastered with cement and either Bermúdez or the family write the name of the deceased and an epitaph on it and bring flowers.

This isn't an ordinary job, or a traditional one. Most people would see it as dark or dreary, but Bermúdez says that she has been brought up with the dead.

Her father was the security guard of Riohacha's central cemetery and she recalls skipping school to spend time with him. It was there, in her teens, that she witnessed how the bodies of the poor and unclaimed were simply dumped in the communal grave, and it irked her. Still in her teens, she won a scholarship to travel to Bogotá to become a coroner. A dream come true!

Once back in Riohacha, she practised her trade by day and buried corpses of the unnamed and destitute in the invaded plot by night. When she had money, she built them coffins. When she didn't, she wrapped them in plastic bags. But never without identifying them by their ID numbers, just in case someone came to claim them.

Bermúdez's cemetery was legalized in 2014 and she now receives funding from local and international organizations, although the costs are often greater than the budgets, which is draining her personal pockets.

Colombia has an estimated population of 1.7 million Venezuelan refugees and migrants, putting huge pressure on the public services of the country, including services for the dead. But Bermúdez promises to not allow a single Venezuelan who dies in La Guajira to be buried without dignity, whatever it takes.

'The satisfaction comes from the fact that a family knows where their loved one is . . . that their loved ones are cared for. This is a way of building peace,' says Bermúdez, her purpose of serving kindness to the deceased deep set in the lines on her face and hands.

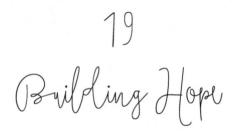

19
Building Hope

**HOW A SIMPLE IFTAR TURNED
INTO A MISSION**

Saudi Arabia

As the saying goes, a journey of a thousand miles begins with a single step. And for the ten co-founders of Ihyaa, it all began with a single meal.

It was the month of Ramadan in the summer of 2015, when ten friends, all students and young professionals, got together to celebrate the holy month to serve Iftar—the evening meal with which Muslims break their fast after nightfall—at the local community in the economically disadvantaged districts of Jeddah.

'The simple act taught us that true happiness is in giving, not in receiving since we are born to serve others,' says Yusof

Othman, about the enterprise they would eventually build to support social projects and empower people.

Bayan Hallak says that the ten friends found the act of serving so meaningful that they just could not go back to their usual lives.

They began ideating on ways they could give more to the community and in a way that had larger and more long-term impact. They realized that communities like the ones they met in Jeddah were not progressing, and immediately recognized that education was the solution and the most sustainable way to produce the kind of impact they hoped to achieve. 'We started Ihyaa as an initiative to use our knowledge and professional background in architecture to serve the widest range of beneficiaries,' recalls Basel Turjuman. And that's how they decided to begin with a summer project renovating a school in the Al-Jamea district.

'I came to believe that serving the people in need is the best way to practice true architecture. I feel very grateful to be part of this life changing initiative because it has taught me skills that I would have never been able to learn in any book, and most importantly because I got the chance to do good deeds for a living,' Adwa AlShammasi shares.

'The fact is that renovating schools does not only affect the buildings but also the students' hopes and dreams and elevate the community that they live in,' explains Afnan AlHalees.

'The effects seen through the school renovation to students and teachers were marvellous, charging us with great energy to thrive for more projects to work on and more students to indulge in education,' recalls Sara AlJabi.

With requests from nearby schools pouring in for renovations, they knew they couldn't stop.

They decided to name the initiative Ihyaa, which means 'to revive' in Arabic, representing their mission to revive and empower the community through education and inspire the youth to serve the community. 'Ihya'a is a name true to itself. It revived in us the beautiful humanity, the love of goodness for others, the love of giving and the love of charity. We dealt with good-hearted people. We worked hard and diligently, and we faced difficulties that we overcame through goodness and work. And, eventually, we won!' Afnan Kahla expresses.

Over the last six years, Ihyaa has completed forty-one initiatives, including eight school renovations, with the help of over 650 volunteers, who clocked in over 20,000 volunteering hours and impacted more than 4100 beneficiaries. 'Ihyaa taught me that having a noble community service goal will touch people's eagerness to give and will gather generous resources you can never acquire otherwise,' shares Hasan CheikhZain. And the impact was not only on the beneficiaries but also on the people working every day to support this cause as Sara AbulHamail adds, 'Ihyaa Group has drastically changed my life in a way I could never imagine.'

Although their group started with ten architects and engineers volunteering on part-time basis, Ihyaa was legally registered as an independent social enterprise in 2020, with two of the founding members even having quit their corporate jobs to pursue this full-time. Today, Ihyaa provides professional corporate social responsibility services with a focus on community development through education and empowerment, and even expanded to offer architectural services that directly supports sustaining their social cause.

And Ihyaa is only growing.

As with Crown Prince Mohammed bin Salman's Saudi Vision 2030, which includes enhancing education, encouraging socially responsible organizations and raising volunteering rates among the community, the initiative has seen not only growth but also support.

'Changing the world might seem impossible but supporting a few students here and there will soon add up to creating more empowered communities. Be the change you want to see in the world—just take the first step and you'll be surprised by the doors you can unlock,' shares Samira Taye.

'You will be showered with blessings when sharing', reads one of the values of Ihyaa. The collective power that the initiative has generated in the community, which started with a simple act of kindness, is a powerful example of how the circle of kindness, once entered, leads to more kindness, both received and given.

* This story was adapted from an article originally published on Goodnet.org, a kindness collaborator of UNESCO MGIEP.

20

Scouting for Joy

**AN ADOPTED BOY'S JOURNEY TO GIVE
BACK TO HIS FIRST HOME**

Russia/United States

Alex Griffith was all of eleven months old when he was adopted by Dwight and Jenny Griffith from the L.S. Berzon City Clinical Hospital No. 20 for abandoned children in the Siberian city of Krasnoyarsk. Sergey, as he was originally named, weighed less than 2 pounds, was malnourished and had hernia, rickets and a mild case of cerebral palsy, the doctors said. His father recalled how his son neither smiled nor moved.

But things started to change for this young boy once he moved to the United States under the care of his new family.

He grew healthier and even joined the Boy Scout, moving up the ranks over the years.

In fact, it was while working to earn the rank of Eagle Scout—the highest scouting honour—that the fourteen-year-old thought of the Krasnoyarsk Playground Project.

The idea came to him when he found the journal his parents had kept from when they travelled to Krasnoyarsk to first meet him. They detailed their thoughts about the hospitals and the adoption process of frail little Alex. They'd also included photos of the hospital, with wards filled with children playing games and riding cycles in the hallways. One of the photos was of the run-down playground with a rusty swing and a sandbox filled with mud—the only outdoor recreation that the kids had.

When Griffith found out that the playground was just the same, even though fourteen years had gone by, he decided to do something about it. And so commenced the Krasnoyarsk Playground Project.

Earning the rank of an Eagle Scout involves service to the community. Ordinarily, boy scouts choose a project close to home and help out at their local church or school or other local services, but not for Griffith, who decided to take up a community project thousands of miles away from his home in Jarrettsville—with the aim to give the children in Hospital No. 20 a proper playground. For the North Harford High School student, it was the place that gave him a life and a chance to survive, and he wanted to give back to his first home.

Mike Balog, Harford County's Eagle Project co-coordinator, believes that this act of kindness has broadened the idea of community to include the entire world.

It took Griffith two and a half years, a total of 500 volunteers across five countries, 2000 volunteer hours, well over 300 emails to forty-five cities across the globe and $60,000—for which he worked with local rotary clubs and collaborated with boy scouts for candy sales, car washes and barbeque fundraisers—to complete the project.

He also worked closely with a manufacturing company to select the components in red, white and blue, all of which were first assembled by him and the team before being shipped to Krasnoyarsk—a trip that took about forty-five days by ship and train. Once in Krasnoyarsk, Alex, his father and ten volunteers put together the swings, rock wall, climbing bridge and 5-foot zip slides. They also installed two 8-foot wooden totem poles carved with an eagle and a bear to symbolize his two homes, to flag the entrance of Hospital No. 20.

Griffith hoped for the project to link all the people who were involved and have been touched by the project in a positive way and it has done so successfully for young ones like Sonja Sultanova, who talks about sliding her sadness away in the playground.

21

Urgently Needed

**A WOMAN'S DRIVE TO HELP THE WORLD
HEAL THROUGH ACTS OF KINDNESS**

United Kingdom

#299 Annie.

Request: Donations for carpet, a seizure monitor and kind messages—reads the 52 Lives home page. Six-year-old Annie has a rare form of cerebral palsy. She can't walk or talk and usually moves around by crawling on her tummy, which is very dangerous given the worn-out and thin carpet in their home that allows for nails from the floor to poke out. Annie often suffers from seizures at night—she was found blue and unresponsive by her mum one morning. The charity, founded in 2013, is helping young Annie and her family out by amplifying their needs and finding a means to get them what they need.

Since its launch, 52 Lives has helped almost 10,000 people all over the world with a variety of things like buying teeth for a man who had none, building a sensory shed for a toddler who was losing her sight, redecorating a little girl's bedroom who had lost her mum, making video messages for a boy who was being bullied, paying for a life-saving operation for a teenager and helping a mother and son get off the streets.

And it all began with an 'Urgently Needed: Rugs' ad on a classified website by a young mum who was looking to cover her broken floor so her children wouldn't cut their feet running around.

'I didn't have a rug, but I emailed her to offer to collect a rug if anyone donated one,' says Jaime Thurston, founder and CEO of 52 Lives. 'The more I learnt about her, the more I wanted to help.' The mother had escaped terrible domestic circumstances with her children and, after a period of homelessness that included living in a garden shed, had finally found a home.

Thurston's family and friends ended up collecting a lot of things for the mum, and the day Thurston brought them to her, the lady was overwhelmed—not because of the things she had received but because, for the first time in a long time, she didn't feel alone. Thurston, too, found herself overwhelmed, but it was a high she'd never felt before. Later, when she learnt more about the science behind the way she felt, she learnt that it was a high of kindness.

Kindness changes our body chemistry, she found. It helps us feel happier, reduces blood pressure, helps relieve pain because it encourages the production of endorphins, slows ageing and, of course, improves relationships. Above all, kindness begets kindness. Studies show that an act of kindness actually creates a ripple effect that spreads outwards to our friends' friends' friends. This means that one act of kindness will positively affect up to 125 people!

It was the kindness 'buzz' that led Thurston to set up 52 Lives and create a Facebook page for it.

'I wanted to do more!' says Thurston, her generous smile spread wide across her glowing face.

Thurston thought that the Facebook page would be a way for her family and friends to help people in need. But today, it is a global movement of almost 1,00,000 people with a corporate sponsor and a proud USP of using 100 per cent of what they get to help people. Thurston is so committed to the initiative that she even used the prize money she got for winning the 2016 Clarins Most Dynamisante Woman of the Year to launch the School of Kindness where they run Kindness Workshops in primary schools every week.

'Kindness improves our physical and mental health, whether we're receiving, giving or even just witnessing kindness. It is such a powerful force for change, and determines the kind of world we have,' says Thurston, describing the tenet on which she has built 52 Lives.

22

Één, Twee, Drie

AN ENVIRONMENTAL CHAMPION RIDDING THE OCEANS OF PLASTIC, ONE PIECE AT A TIME

Netherlands

'Één, twee, drie, vier . . . achtenvijftig, negenenvijftig, zestig . . .'
Lilly Platt trailed off.

It was a beautiful day in Voorschoten, Netherlands, and Lilly and her grandpa had decided to take a walk to a McDonald's nearby for burgers. On their way there, Lilly spotted a piece of plastic. But she made nothing of it and walked ahead. Then she saw another one, and two, and three and four.

Born in the United Kingdom, the seven-year-old had just moved to the Netherlands and was still learning her Dutch on that day. So her grandpa suggested that Lilly should practise her counting on the plastics she found littered on their way while he told her all about their life cycle.

He told her about the 'plastic soup'—how the plastic disintegrates into microplastic, makes its way to the oceans and into the stomachs of planktons that are eaten by the fish that are then eaten by the bigger fish, which are finally eaten by humans. Lilly's eyes grew bigger in wonder. No one wants to eat that soup!

She wasn't sure if she should be mad or sad, so she decided to do something about it instead.

In that fifteen-minute walk, Lilly counted ninety-one pieces of plastic. To think that all of those would be in the oceans!

She decided she wouldn't let another piece of plastic be strewn around her and thus began Lilly's Plastic Pickup.

'I knew that every piece I picked up was one less piece that could harm a living creature,' the kind Lilly chats, going a mile a minute.

This was in 2015. Since then, Lilly has become a leading advocate for cleaning up plastic pollution, restricting plastic production and finding alternatives to the material, *and* picked up nearly 2,00,000 pieces of plastic!

Every plastic she picks is meticulously sorted into groups— canned goods, bottles, glass—and sent for recycling.

But given the scale of the problem, she knows she cannot beat it alone. That is why she now spends a lot of her time raising awareness. She photographs every piece of plastic she collects and puts it up on social media along with challenges and incentives for people to fight plastic pollution.

She urges everyone to pick up at least three pieces of plastic a day. 'Even though it may be small, if everyone did that, it would be a huge help for the planet,' she says, holding everyone's attention with her energy as she speaks about our role in showing kindness to the planet.

She also organizes beach clean-ups and gives presentations in schools in the hope to inspire kids like her.

And so she has!

But even with the community behind her, she is convinced that the real solution lies in pressurizing politicians to ban plastic, which starts by influencing the results in the ballot box. To make sure she took the first step towards this solution too, she got her grandpa to pledge his vote to her for the coming elections so she could pick a candidate who had plans of strong green initiatives.

'Because I wasn't of age to vote for someone that does great things for the planet, my grandpa actually voted for me and for the candidate of my choice, so I had a voice,' she says. 'Then we made a video about that.'

She asks other kids to do the same and get their parents, uncles and grandparents to give them their vote.

Lilly has been chosen as a Youth Ambassador for the Plastic Pollution Coalition and a World Oceans Day Italy (WODI), HOW Global, YouthMundus, Earth.Org. Her activism now extends beyond plastic pollution. She also talks about and campaigns for wildlife conservation, indigenous rights and climate action. In her latest campaign, she urges everyone to cultivate a 'green heart', which entails people sharing stories about the environment they live in and the environment they want with the hope that politicians will listen and take action.

'You are important, you are needed and together we can save the world!' Lilly ends, swinging her hands as she urges children to speak up and start now, even if it is with the simple act of picking up litter they spot, one piece at a time.

LADYBIRD LIFE

DJ Elton
(Australia)

Monday, in the kitchen, chopping some spinach
Dark green, luscious crinkled
Checking more carefully than usual for bugs.
    My friend likes organic.
I encountered you. All golden with brown spots.
    Not red.
I thought you could be dead but
You slipped on to my finger ever so gently and
The kindness in me decided to take you outside
To munch on the tomato plant.
Windy day with sunshine brightly, the tomatoes did
    not seem a fitting home for you,
Not looking like a forest, standing in their
    plastic pots.
I took you further, past the cactus to the red-green
    leaved tree.
Don't know its name. And I wasn't even sure then
If you were dead or play-acting,
But you certainly grounded to my finger and slowly
One by one little thin legs emerged. You moved
As I tried to rest you on the fresh leaves, a splendid
    breakfast.

But you wouldn't budge off my finger.
You clung to my skin and finally
You leapt up, swelling in your shell and flew off
Into the fairyland of our back garden
Leaving me with memories and a poem.
(Spillwords Press)

* Curated by *The Alipore Post*

Kindness

is a language

the deaf can hear

and the blind can see

23

Together We Glow

**AN AFRICAN SOCIAL ENTREPRENEUR
FIGHTING GENDER EQUALITY**

Malawi

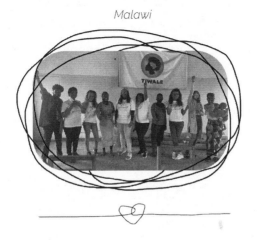

The United Nations' Global Sustainable Development Goal (SDG) 5 aims to fight all forms of discrimination and harmful practices against girls and women, achieve gender equality and empower them with equal opportunities.

Globally, 750 million women and girls were married before the age of eighteen. Projections before the pandemic showed that more than 200 million children would be out of school, and only 60 per cent of young people would be completing upper secondary education in 2030. After that, the figures are estimated to be much higher. In 2016, some 750 million adults remained illiterate, two-thirds of them were women.

In Malawi, figures from a 2019 report by the World Bank indicate that female enrolment in secondary schools was only 33.7 per cent. In fact, their percentage of primary school completion for women is also one of the lowest in the world.

This lack of education is one of the key factors that adds to the poverty and gender disparity in Malawi. And in response to this crisis in her hometown, the Forbes 30 Under 30 entrepreneur, Chmba Ellen Chilemba, founded Tiwale when she was seventeen years old.

Tiwale, meaning 'let's glow' in Chichewa, is a community-based organization in Malawi that works with women and gender-expansive folks to empower them to develop sustainable ventures and provide them with access to educational and economic opportunities. The motive is to enable them to break the cycle of poverty and child marriage.

The idea for the project was first conceived when fifteen-year-old Chilemba witnessed her friend being forced out of school and into child marriage. 'In that moment, I recognized the severity of systematic inequality against girls and people of colour globally,' Chilemba recalls.

At sixteen, when Chilemba was offered a scholarship to attend the African Leadership Academy in South Africa, she knew she had just landed an opportunity to study leadership and that she needed to spark her activism. Combined with the values of kindness and humanity taught to her by her parents, she launched Tiwale a year later in 2012.

The focus of the organization was on microlending in the beginning. She helped girls who lived in poverty fund their own education by helping them set up a source of income. However, Chilemba soon hit a roadblock; she hadn't considered the girls who did not have time to run businesses when they had to shoulder responsibilities at schools and at home.

So Chilemba got back to ideating.

'You have to be open to being corrected,' Chilemba says. And she knew that there was no better way to correct that than involving the community and inviting feedback.

She quickly changed tack and now works primarily with women who are unemployed or homemakers to provide vocational training and school grants for those who would like to go back to school. They also have an educational programme that assists with homework, a microfinance programme that includes a business education workshop and $70 interest-free loans for the best business plans by the end of it.

Tiwale is a hybrid enterprise, a non-profit with for-profit activities to fund the community, and Chilemba a very smart businesswoman. One of the central vocational trainings that the initiative runs is that of tie-dye. When Chilemba saw that many women in Malawi wore bright dyed clothing but most of it was imported, she knew it was a potential business. She began training women in the craft and now sells the cloth to the designers and directly online as tapestries and tote bags. The women are allowed to keep 60 per cent of the profit and 40 per cent goes back into the company to help train more women and perpetuate the cycle.

Keeping up with the trends and the rising demand for African music, Tiwale has expanded its class offerings to include DJing and music production.

What started as a small team of five teenagers and a microfinancing programme has now impacted 396 women and girls and reached over 22,000 young people.

Chilemba herself has won many awards, including being named a Bill and Melinda Gates Foundation Goalkeeper, Global Citizen Youth Advocate, One Young World Ambassador and Commonwealth Awardee for Excellence in Development.

And there is a lot more to come from the young girl who has big plans, with innovation and listening at its heart. 'I want a world where people live more freely,' she says. 'I hope by living honestly I am inspiring a younger person to do the same.'

24

The Lego Grandma

**MAKING LEGO FOR PEOPLE
OF ALL ABILITIES**

Germany

The room is filled with laughter and Lego as Rita Ebel works at her kitchen table to complete the portrait of Olaf the Snowman to match that of Elsa the snow queen, both from *Frozen*. Her husband Wolfgang stands over her, squirting with the glue gun as she carefully places the Lego pieces, making sure they are firmly in place. It will take 6–8 hours of combined work and 7–8 kg of Lego to complete.

But this is no ordinary art that the sixty-four-year-old is doing. Five-year-old Mona suffers from the rare hereditary spastic paraplegia, a condition that causes progressive weakness and spasticity of the legs, confining her to a wheelchair. She can get around independently with a wheelchair, but the only barrier is the one step at the main entrance to her home. Ebel's ramp fits right in here, allowing Mona to be completely independent.

Ebel herself has been wheelchair bound for over twenty-six years after a car accident left her with incomplete paralysis. For someone who has always been very active, this was a shock.

'The worst part was being dependent on others. I wanted to get back to doing a lot of things myself as soon as possible,' Ebel says, her bright smile matching her golden bob.

Over the years, she taught herself to walk short distances on crutches with the help of physical therapists, but her biggest step toward independence was making and installing Lego ramps in her hometown of Hanau, Germany.

Ebel began building these ramps in 2019 when a friend, who also relies on a wheelchair, complained that she couldn't leave a store in town and had to be carried out by her friends. Always positive, Ebel decided to find a solution, which she finally came up with when she read an article about Corinna Huber in a medical journal. Huber, who had built Lego ramps in another part of Germany, was happy to provide Ebel with instructions on how to build her own.

By early 2020, Ebel had already built twenty ramps, not only for businesses in her city and for children with disabilities but also to send to other parts of Germany, Switzerland, Austria and Italy.

'The ramps are super sturdy, can be built for different heights, and have the advantage of being mobile and grippy,' says Ebel, who has since been dubbed 'Lego Grandma'.

Her twenty-first ramp has the height of two stairs, a first for Ebel! She is also in talks with the Spanish Tourism Board to collaborate on its plan to make travel accessible for all.

Getting there, however, has not been without challenges.

For starters, each ramp requires 7000–8000 Lego pieces. And given the high cost of Lego and Ebel's desire to always give the ramps away for free, sourcing Lego was difficult.

'Lego is something that goes through all generations, so people often don't want to give it away. And when they do, the parts often aren't suitable for my ramps,' Ebel says in her Hessian accent.

Another challenge is that Ebel's ramps are not officially classified as wheelchair ramps in Germany because the laws only allow a slope of 6 per cent. That means a ramp must be several metres long to negotiate a 15 cm step, and that's not always possible because the sidewalk doesn't provide enough space. In Munich, this has led to the city council forcing some store owners to remove the ramps.

Of course, there's also the kindness Ebel finds in people like the online retailer who unhesitatingly sent her two large boxes of Lego to build her first ramp, the many who now donate Lego to her, and others in her neighbourhood who now store boxes of it for her. And then there are people like the mayor of her hometown, who supported her idea even though it didn't meet German requirements for a wheelchair ramp.

'For me, it's about making the world a little more aware of accessibility,' Ebel says. And the colourful ramp, many with their own artwork, which Ebel calls eye-catchers, is the perfect, creative way to do just that—draw attention to the insurmountable obstacles that exist for people with disabilities, in wheelchairs, with strollers or walkers. There are now already fifty-four ramps.

'There is no situation that is only bad. We all have to find even the small good in the negative,' says Ebel, who has already sent out more than 500 instructions on how to build ramps in nine different languages to anyone who wants to build one themselves.

* This story was adapted from an article originally published on Goodnet.org, a kindness collaborator of UNESCO MGIEP.

25

On Board

**AN ORGANIZATION USING SKATEBOARD
TO HELP KIDS EXCEL**

Cambodia

Kouv Chamsangva, fondly called Tin, was only six when she knew with certainty that she wanted to become a teacher with an NGO. Having a physically abusive father cemented in her the need to help children like her receive quality education and a life away from violence.

In 2012, Tin took the first step towards realizing her dream when she joined Skateistan Cambodia, an NGO that uses skateboarding for development and as a bridge to empower and educate children in a fun and interactive environment.

The initiative was started in 2008 by Australian skateboarder Oliver Percovich, who was visiting Afghanistan as a university researcher. Percovich was skating through the streets of Kabul when he noticed the fascination with which children regarded his skateboard. He kindly lent his skateboards to three of them, and seeing how much they enjoyed using them, he started running informal skating classes near an out-of-use fountain.

A few kids soon became hundreds from different ethnic and economic backgrounds. There were a lot of girls too, which, given Afghanistan's social norms that do not allow girls from engaging in sports activities, was surprising (skateboarding was allowed as it was considered a toy)!

Percovich immediately saw an opportunity to bring about well-rounded development in a war-torn Afghanistan and opened Skateistan in 2009. The first skate school in Kabul offered multiple programmes, which were integrated to create a holistic curriculum steeped in kindness and understanding towards the children, all of whom come from diverse backgrounds, physical capabilities and economic conditions.

The Outreach programme currently brings Skateistan educators to children with limited resources, introduces new communities to skateboarding and develops partnerships to connect young people and their families to volunteer services.

The Skate and Create programme also helps students build life skills through a balance of social sports and structured learning with the aim to provide a safe space for young people of all levels of literacy and ability and promote confidence, resilience, equality, creative expression and skill-based knowledge.

The Back-to-School programme partners with schools to align their students to the national curriculums and helps support them through public education.

The Dropping In programme provides learning spaces and resources where students can develop their aspirations and realize their potential.

Finally, motivated students like Tin are invited to join the Youth Leadership programme to become more involved in developing their community through Skateistan.

At eighteen, Tin started to volunteer with Skateistan Cambodia as a teacher, which had been started in Phnom Penh by Benjamin Pecqueur in 2011. Pecqueur had already been running skateboard classes for children there when he heard of Skateistan and contacted the Kabul centre in hopes of starting a school in the capital. He was the country manager of Skateistan Cambodia whereas Tin is the general manager, in charge of the finance, human resources and development and communications departments. 'I was lucky that Skateistan chose me to work with them. I wanted to change the opinion of the community that girls couldn't do things. Now I'm one of the best female skaters in Cambodia and have become a role model for girls who want to skate,' Tin says, who has been with the NGO for over ten years.

Skateistan currently has three skate schools in Afghanistan, one in Phnom Penh, one in Johannesburg and a newly opened one in Jordan with a focus on groups that are often excluded from sport and educational opportunities like girls, children with disabilities and children from low-income families. The schools also run special programmes for girls and children with disabilities to make them feel safe and encouraged.

Skateistan has also inspired people across the globe with their work, like Ulrike Reinhard who started Janwaar Castle with the aim to give kids in rural India a chance to simply have fun while learning new skills and gain self-confidence.

'There is no wrong or right way to skate. We don't mind if a child wants to sit on the board instead of standing on it. We are not trying to create the next generation of pro skateboarders, we are trying to create a safe space where everyone is included,' concludes Tin, reflecting the kind approach to healing and growth that the initiative fosters, not only through its inclusive curriculum but also patient and understanding teaching practices.

* This story was adapted from an article originally published on Goodnet.org, a kindness collaborator of UNESCO MGIEP.

A COMMITMENT TO *kindness* CAN CREATE

BIG

IMPACT

26

Ammu

**A WOMAN'S FIGHT TO CHANGE THE FATE
OF CHILDREN OF SEX WORKERS**

Bangladesh

Hazera Begum was all of seven when she ran away from home after a clash with her stepmother. Her own mother had died giving birth to her younger brother. Her father, a fisherman incapable of feeding his children, had to remarry. But the stepmother refused to give them food or care. Unable to tolerate her any longer, Hazera fled, fell asleep on a bus and woke up on the other end of Dhaka, in Gulistan.

For the next few years, as she made her way as a street child, she was bought and sold many times, first for domestic work and finally, at the age of eleven, for prostitution.

Life continued to be nightmarish for Hazera, who worked as a sex worker in brothels and on the streets until the age of twenty-three.

Things finally began to take a turn for the better for her when she encountered someone from CARE, an international non-profit organization. An industrious woman, Hazera had over the years tried her best to skill herself in crafts and pick up basic education, and she quickly managed to get a job with them.

It was Durjoy, another organization for sex workers, which set Hazera off on her journey of working with children of sex workers. Under the Durjoy project, she was given the responsibility of taking care of children of sex workers and over time, she began to form an affinity with them. So, when the funded child centre run by Durjoy shut down, she frantically began to find a way to take care of these kids and give them a future. While she never wanted to have a child of her own, she worried for the kind of future she'd be able to give them. She was determined to care for the ones around her.

'I told myself that I will do something for these kids so that they can do what I could not,' says Hazera.

With the contribution of a few students of Jahangirnagar University and her life savings of about 8,00,000 taka (approximately $10,000), she started Shishuder Jonno Aamra (SJA), which translates to 'we are for the children', and registered it with the government's Social Welfare Department.

The shelter began in June 2010 in Savar, a suburb of the capital, with twenty-five children. Then in 2011, the shelter was shifted to Adabar area of the capital Dhaka.

Most girls living with their mothers in the sex trade end up being part of the trade themselves, while the boys often resort to a life of drug trade and extortion. Hazera's aim was to change this by making sure the girls completed their higher education and boys were trained in vocations for better job opportunities as electricians, drivers and more.

But the challenge has been far greater. Many opposed her vision. Institutes refused to enrol the children simply because they came from the brothels, but Hazera refused to give up. Slowly, things started to improve.

Today, Hazera is the mother of forty-six children, and her initiative is being run primarily by donations from some humanitarian people, some students, three trust organizations and one charity organization. Although the organization (SJA) is registered with the government's social welfare department, they are not receiving any government donations.

'She is not just my mother; she is my best friend,' said Fatema, a fourth-grade student who came to the shelter in 2013.

Like Fatema, all other children are extremely fond of Hazera, who dotes on each one of them equally (although she does admit to taking extra care of her daughters, especially after they have grown up).

With the expense of renting and growing the shelter in the capital, Hazera now endeavours to buy a larger space so she can bring in more children.

Hazera's kindness is reflected in the love that she receives from not only the children who call her Ammu but also their biological mothers and everyone else whose lives she has touched. As the biological mother of one of Hazera's children puts it, 'I gave birth, so what? The one who takes care is far greater.'

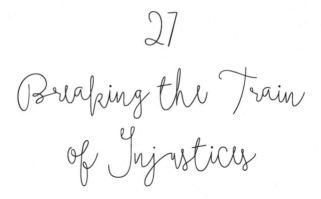

27
Breaking the Train
of Injustices

AN INTERVIEW WITH MARTIN KARADZHOV

Bulgaria

Martin Karadzhov (he/him) is a queer feminist activist, movement builder and writer from Bulgaria committed towards working on intersectionality and systemic inequalities.

He has worked in the fields of sexual and reproductive health, comprehensive sexuality education (CSE), HIV, domestic violence prevention and LGBTIQ issues. He is currently a board member of ILGA World, the largest global federation of LGBTI organizations; chair of the first global LGBTI youth steering committee; a member of YouAct, the European youth network for sexual and reproductive health and rights (SRHR); and the founder of the Global Queer Youth Network.

How did you develop an interest in the work that you do?

I was thirteen when my biology teacher asked me if I would like to volunteer with an NGO working to promote CSE. There was no sex education in Bulgaria, where I was born and raised, at the time. There still isn't, and there are NGOs that work with children in schools and outside of them—in shelters with juvenile offenders and young people with disabilities—to provide them with CSE.

In the beginning, I said yes because it was simply about connecting with people. I lived away from my family and wanted to find my own community. Over time, however, I recognized that I had an inherent desire to work towards correcting injustices around domestic violence, sexual health and LGBTIQ rights.

Was there any personal encounter that triggered this burning desire to work towards correcting these injustices?

My mother is a Christian. My dad was a Bulgarian Muslim—a Pomak—an ethnic minority in the country. The cultural and social injustices that we saw being meted out to him throughout his life affected even his last days, in getting treatment in a hospital! Attacks on human rights come hand in hand or one after another. When we are silent on one attack, we are not only complicit in it but are also encouraging other injustices in turn.

And you are now actively working in the LGBTIQ space . . .

This, too, goes back to experiences growing up. As a closeted queer young person, I didn't find the environment or find people and communities whom I could engage with. I only recently realized that I cannot relate to the CSE that I volunteered to provide to so many fellow children because it doesn't include LGBTIQ. We thought there was so much in it that was innovative and advanced for its time but it was quite heteronormative.

Now I understand that comprehensive sexuality education is only comprehensive when it includes the LGBTIQ community, otherwise it's only sex education. And I want to work towards fixing that and towards giving the community a face and voice. In fact, this sense of injustice never leaves you. It only motivates you to change things and do things differently.

Would you say that the work you're doing towards bringing about change in the world is an act of kindness?

I've never seen my volunteer work as kindness. I can understand why it may seem like it to people, but for me it's simply the drive to stop the train of injustices in the way I can do best. I don't remember a time when I wasn't like this; I can't just sit and watch. I have always taken injustice of all kinds personally and it comes from a place of care and being hyper connected and hyper perceptive.

And what's next on your agenda?

The optimistic goal is to campaign to banish all attacks and harmful practices against the LGBTIQ community by the end of this decade. We hope to do this by integrating the queer community in decision-making processes. Young people are not represented when decisions about their own future are made, and queer young people are found ever lesser. We aim to change that, starting with the launch of the Global Queer Youth Network, an organization I've founded to provide the community a safe space to speak up. We are running a twelve-month Queer Youth Dialogue, with the UN, that brings together queer youth activists and organizations to engage in conversation and create a strong global queer youth movement. Of course, my day job as the London coordinator at the LGBT+ consortium, the managerial roles with ILGA and the advocacy on reproductive rights with YouAct would continue.

Eventually, Karadzhov also wants to integrate his study of Theatre in Education with his volunteer work and use creative spaces to work with human rights. He has done so earlier through games, role play and forum theatre to raise awareness about CSE, consent and violence against women amongst the youth in Bulgaria, but believes that there is great potential in integrating social justice and the arts. Until then, he has only one urgent request to all youth: 'Say yes to those opportunities in your cities and countries and work with non-profit organizations and charities. One person facing injustice is an injustice to everyone, and we all need to work to change that.'

28

Of Rainbows and Revolution

**GIVING MARGINALIZED COMMUNITIES
SAFE SPACES IN MANIPUR**

India

Stigma, discrimination and a lack of social support and safe spaces for interactions have left queer youth across the world unable to come out or seek help. The situation is no different in the state of Manipur. A conflicted border state, it has other issues that it prioritizes like the citizenship crisis, insurgency, militarization, substance abuse, unemployment, migration, high HIV prevalence and high school dropout rate, leaving its youth, especially the queer community, struggling to meet daily needs and wanting for help.

Sadam Hanjabam was one of them. 'Growing up in Imphal, we saw violence and death at our doorstep routinely. But I told myself there were always more important things going on, bigger things to worry about.'

Hanjabam grew up afraid of not just the violence outside but, having been inside the closet since a young age, fearful of the turmoil inside of him too.

Often, for the queer youth in Manipur, migration is the way out, a way to seek liberation, explore their sexual identity and earn a living. For the ones who cannot afford to migrate, the obscurity of identity and sexual orientation continue to have a direct impact on their mental well-being and basic survival.

Luckily for Hanjabam, he was able to migrate for his higher education. He travelled from Assam to Kerala before moving to Mumbai—the city he had seen on television and dreamt of being in—for his MPhil.

It was here that he was able to express, and even celebrate, being queer for the first time. He began using dating apps and meeting men, going on dates and becoming part of a larger queer community.

But his troubles were far from over.

In Mumbai, he faced discrimination of a different kind. 'I did not look like someone from Manipur because I am not fair and my eyes are a little wider,' recalls Hanjabam. For many, he became the 'Nepali'. For others, he became the Muslim whom they couldn't rent their house to.

After months of couch-surfing at the hostel rooms of friends, he changed his surname, using his father's 'Sharma', and finally managed to rent a room. But a sense of rejection settled into him.

Perhaps it was this constant feeling of being alone and forcing himself to take up the scholarship and pursue a PhD simply to escape going back to Manipur, but when a partner he met on a dating app suggested they try having 'high fun', he agreed.

One night turned into two, and smoking turned to snorting and even injecting. Soon Hanjabam became an addict who would find himself in cycles of overdosing, recovering and relapsing for years to come.

But it all changed when he learnt of a friend dying from an overdose while he lay in the psychiatric ward of a hospital after overdosing once again. Hanjabam realized that he had barely escaped death twice himself. He decided to let go of his fears and come clean to the doctors.

'I told them about not being sure of wanting to do my PhD, about my struggles to fit in and about how I was a queer man.' Soon after, he looked for a queer-affirmative counsellor and began his journey of accepting himself with all the vulnerabilities and strength.

The experience in the hospital struck a chord with Hanjabam who recognized the critical need for a safe space where one can indulge in honest expression without fear of judgement or rejection, especially for the queer community that is often marginalized.

That is how Ya-All ('revolution' in Manipuri) began on the International Day Against Homophobia, Transphobia and

Biphobia as a secret WhatsApp group in 2017. It tried to initiate conversation about the issues faced by queer youth in Manipur—substance abuse that is rampant in the state due to its proximity to the 'Golden Triangle', known for illegal drug trading in the world; accessibility to sexual and mental healthcare; and employment. The group came out openly as a collective soon after and has since been working to help promote safe spaces for the queer community in Manipur.

Ya-All has set up Meitram, a space aimed to destigmatize conversations around queer issues and empower and equip the youth with a co-working space; and partnered with Mariwala Health Initiative, which has helped them create a mental health space for queer youths with free peer counselling. They have also collaborated with Blued, a gay dating app, to report crimes like online bullying and extortion, which is often seen in cases of substance abuse within the queer community; and brought together India's first transgender football team.

'My father raised me like a boy, and when he found out that I was a part of India's first transgender football team, he was proud of me,' says vice-captain Chaoba Wahengbam, who used to play in the women's category earlier. 'My mother used to scold me because society used to mock her, but after the acknowledgement our team received, she accepted me as I am.'

Hanjabam has turned to kindness as a driving force in all his endeavours since his recovery, whether it is working to include a football team of transgender players, crowdfunding to support people with ration during the pandemic, distributing condoms and sanitary pads, supporting Manipur students who were racially abused due to the pandemic or assisting people through telephonic counselling. 'Only once we accept our vulnerabilities can we find ways to turn them into our biggest strengths,' he concludes.

29

Click for Kindness

**A GEN Z FILM-MAKER ON A MISSION
TO DOCUMENT KINDNESS**

Canada

Fifteen years ago, when eight-year-old Kasha Sequoia Slavner founded her first business of selling home-made sugar scrubs, it marked the beginning of her journey into the world of kindness. A few years later, upon discovering her love for photography, she started a photography card line called Kasha's Cards of Kindness. With every business she launched, Kasha made sure that 50 per cent of the funds she raised was donated to support women's shelters, children's hospital wards, neighbourhood clean-ups and the homeless in her hometown of Toronto.

At fourteen, she was attending her first UN conference on gender equality as the youngest member of Canada's oldest feminist peace organization, The Canadian Voice of Women for Peace, where the incredible stories of women and youth from around the world inspired her. These were people from grassroots organizations who were working on finding sustainable solutions to some of the most daunting issues impacting women and children.

Kasha knew immediately that she wanted to use her ability to capture stories, something she'd honed since launching her photography card line, to motivate social action.

This is when the Global Sunrise Project was born.

Once home, she convinced her mom of her plan to travel the world and document stories of ordinary people who'd triumphed over adversities and extraordinary circumstances to do their bit to bring about a positive change.

Kasha believes that the media often focuses on negative news and conditions us to feel overwhelmed, disempowered and apathetic. With the Global Sunrise Project and the subsequent film it evolved into, *The Sunrise Storyteller*, she aims to turn the spotlight on positive and impactful narratives.

'Giving back has always been at the core of what I do. I have always believed that taking action was the best way to make a difference,' she says.

Coming from a single-parent household, she relied on the kindness of strangers to raise money for the project. It took a while, as many thought of her idea as cute and her as only a fifteen-year-old child, but Kasha finally fundraised enough to be on the road for six months.

The mother-daughter duo travelled to East Africa and Southeast Asia to gather tales of hope and resilience, ending with the story of Canadian Vietnamese napalm bomb survivor Kim Phuc who speaks of forgiveness and peace.

Since the release of the film in 2017, it has been screened at sixty film festivals and won thirty awards, including the Ron Kovic Peace Prize.

'Giving others hope is an act of kindness,' says the now twenty-three-year-old, her dancing fringe matching her enthusiastic smile. And she hopes that the stories she tells through her photography, film and words inspire people to get involved in humanitarian problems and understand what it means to be a global citizen.

Her next film, *1.5 Degrees of Peace*, explores the link between peace and climate movements past and present, through inspiring stories of young climate and peace activists working on the front line of these issues.

Today, the Global Sunrise Project is a team of social impact storytellers who work to create alternative narratives that reflect resilience, passion and hope, all with the aim of making the world a better place, one inspiring story at a time.

'Small actions = big change', reads a poster in an early YouTube video on the Global Sunrisers page, and knowing that the self-proclaimed socially anxious film-maker Kasha has initiated such change is an inspiration in itself.

ele

30

It Is about the Finish

AN ATHLETE SETS AN EXAMPLE OF WHAT
TRUE SPORTSMANSHIP IS ABOUT

Guinea-Bissau

A plane ticket in his pocket, Braima Suncar Dabo spends his last minutes back home in Caitó with his family. He will be flying to Portugal with Na Rota dos Povos, a Portuguese organization founded with the aim to promote development through education in the Tombali Region of Guinea-Bissau. He will finish his secondary studies and then graduate from the Polytechnic Institute of Bragança, where he will pursue a management course.

The twenty-six-year-old athlete is busy in conversation, unaware that soon he will be one of the four nominees for the

World Athletics Fair Play Award 2019. That he will win is unfathomable. In fact, it does not even occur to him that he is deserving of the praise that he will receive from the world over, including being named the Honorary Goodwill Ambassador of Aruba. 'Any athlete in that situation would do the same thing,' Dabo says, oblivious of his sportsmanship and kindness that has been making headlines.

Only a few weeks ago, when preparing for the men's 5000 m race of the world track and field championships in Doha where he was representing Guinea-Bissau, Dabo aimed to beat his personal record and represent his country to the best of his abilities. And so he did.

On his last lap, Dabo saw Jonathan Busby of Aruba lean awkwardly, on the verge of collapse, and instinctively slowed down to help his fellow competitor. 'I knew immediately that I had to help him,' Dabo says. He propped Busby up against himself, arms around the shoulder, and helped him around the last turn and across the finish line. Five minutes later, the pair received a standing ovation from the crowd at the Khalifa Stadium.

Busby and Dabo were the only athletes from their nations at the world championships. Both of them competed under special invitations that allowed countries without strong track programs to send one athlete to the championships, even if that athlete had not met qualifying standards.

They travelled all the way to compete so they could finish, and Dabo made sure they did.

Dabo was in the twelfth grade when he first expressed that he wanted to run and participate in the Porto Half Marathon. Until then, nobody in the 'adoptive' family had even noticed him running! But soon, his 'adoptive' mother found a group called Parque da Cidade do Porto for him to join and he began training. Suddenly, everyone realized that he always did run a lot. There was no stopping him now. He never missed training. 'Running makes me feel free!' Dabo says.

Even as he pursues his college degree, he follows a strict training regimen. His day starts at 6.30 a.m. with a race around Bragança. Followed by bath, breakfast, classes, lunch, more classes, late afternoon training, shower, dinner and bed. On Tuesdays and Wednesdays, he manages to squeeze in more training time. On Fridays, he travels back home to be back on Sunday, with long training hours on Saturday.

The plan is to pack the routine with a lot more training, now that he is only left with three more subjects for the course. The aim is to one day compete with world athletes and fight for the podiums.

Knowing Dabo though, even in the competition, he is sure to make friends.

'It's a friendship that will last!' says Dabo, his teeth adding a sparkle to his smile as he talks about his choice to forgo beating his own personal best and helping Busby finish instead. And as you watch Busby look up at his 'brother' as he now calls him, you realize how a simple act of kindness can unite not only people but also countries.

31

The Forest Warrior

**A WOMAN'S TWENTY-YEAR-LONG BATTLE
TO PROTECT HER FOREST**

Peru

The remote north-eastern corner of Loreto, Peru is home to millions of acres of Amazon rainforest—one of the most biodiverse ecosystems on the planet, with over 3000 species of plants, 550 species of fish and 500 species of birds, woolly monkeys, manatees, otters and river dolphins. The tracts of peatland in the forest act as the world's largest carbon sinks and help reverse climate change, while providing safe drinking water and flood control. Twenty-nine indigenous communities live along its borders, one of them being the Bora community.

Liz Chicaje Churay is part of this tiny community and the guardian of this forest. In fact, all the communities living around the forest are its guardians, having inherited it from their ancestors, and all believe that the forest that sustains them and gives them life is sacred.

Which is why, when Chicaje first saw the forest become prey to exploitative activities, she decided to stand up against them to protect her forest. She was only sixteen at the time and became the first activist in her community.

Over the years, as illegal gold mining, overfishing and logging increased, Chicaje joined hands with indigenous leader Benjamin Rodriguez. The two recognized that the only way to protect the forest and its people would be to help get it the status of a national park. And so, the struggle began. They both understood that they couldn't do it alone, so Chicaje set out to bring the locals together to save their land. She visited the twenty-nine communities by boat and persuaded twenty-three to join hands with them.

With these numbers, Chicaje then partnered with NGOs, scientists and conservationists—from as far away as the Field Museum of Chicago, USA and the Frankfurt Zoological Society, Germany—to map out the area and document its biodiversity.

But the biggest challenge was to convince lawmakers, who did not believe in the importance of taking care of forests or understand the realities for the communities living around it, let alone the need for an indigenous-led national park. Starting with the minister of environment and Congress in Lima, Chicaje and Rodriguez travelled around the globe to persuade ambassadors, ministers and lawmakers to listen to them—the people who know the forests best—and support their cause.

Three years later, in 2018, Chicaje and Rodriguez saw their efforts bear fruit as Peru declared the creation of Yaguas National Park, which covered the area of over two million acres, and recognized the rights of the indigenous communities to this land.

In 2021, thirty-eight-year-old Chicaje and Rodriguez were awarded the annual Goldman Environmental Prize, which recognizes grassroots activism. Unfortunately, Rodriguez had passed away due to complications after he contracted Covid-19 in July 2020, but Chicaje continues his legacy, now aiming to keep up the momentum and see global change. Nature is the greatest wealth, Chicaje believes, and the work to preserve the forest and the environment must continue.

32

Educate for Peace

**A MAN'S DETERMINATION TO RID THE
WORLD OF ITS CURRICULUM OF HATE**

Pakistan

Hussain Haider was in the seventh grade when he witnessed
a suicide bombing near his school in Rawalpindi, Pakistan.
When it was revealed that the attacker had been a young
boy of thirteen or fourteen, almost Haider's age, it got Haider
questioning the circumstances in the boy's life that could have
convinced him to take not just his own life but the lives of
perfect strangers too.

The answer came to Haider when he went back home.
It was the lack of education. 'The uneducated youth is an
easy target to exploit,' he says. The knowledge that there

are millions of children in Pakistan who are out of school scared him.

He started performing street theatre to spread awareness about education and peace and initiated a donation drive to collect books for those who didn't have access to them. His theatre performances and use of theatre as a tool for awareness was even recognized by the then prime minister of Pakistan.

Over time, the school-grown project founded by Haider took on the form of Beydaar Society—a youth-led organization that promotes awareness of child abuse, gender equality and reproductive rights; helps children from disadvantaged backgrounds to gain an education; and promotes peace, interfaith harmony and kindness.

'We have to realize that the lack of education is not the problem of one country but a collective problem for the human race. If one country's children don't have access to education, it will directly or indirectly affect other countries,' says Haider.

Like many other organizations run by young people, Haider has struggled to be taken seriously and find support, but the image of the bomb blast he had witnessed and the understanding that educating the youth was the only solution has kept him going.

With various projects under its wings now, Beydaar Society adopts innovative methods and activities like seminars, symposiums, theatre, training sessions, photography, painting, short films, documentaries, essay writing, debates, group discussions, etc., as a tool for youth empowerment and peacebuilding.

Haider himself has taken road trips across Pakistan, stopping in the smallest villages and the biggest cities to convince families to send their children to school; and train communities on education policies, innovative learning methodologies, ways of reopening ghost schools; and designing campaigns to control school dropout numbers. He has fervently campaigned for the exclusion of hate material towards other religions from the national curriculum in Pakistan.

Haider has also co-founded EchoChange, an international platform that brings together young people and youth organizations to promote peace and harmony. Over the years, he has brought together more than 400 youth groups, student societies and youth-led NGOs through this endeavour.

Since starting Beydaar, he has also established a large network of volunteers and ambassadors, trained over 10,000 young leaders across Pakistan, changed hundreds of radicalized or potentially radical minds of Pakistani youth and re-enrolled many children to schools.

'I have come to understand that all religions promote the same human values, and seeking of knowledge had been declared as a religious obligation regardless of gender,' reflects Haider, who is determined to use quality education and dialogue to get rid of the hatred that he believes is intrinsic to the way societies and policies have been operating thus far.

33

Rapping to Freedom

**A YOUNG RAPPER'S CRY AGAINST
BRIDES FOR SALE**

Afghanistan

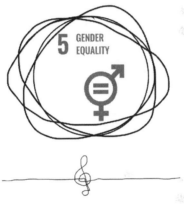

All of sixteen, Sonita Alizadeh lived alone in Tehran and worked as a cleaner while learning how to read and write at an NGO for Afghans like her. Her family of nine had returned to Afghanistan three years ago from Iran, where they'd been forced to flee as refugees. So, when her mother came to visit Alizadeh, in the midst of preparing for her brother's wedding, Alizadeh was overjoyed.

But a few days into the visit, Alizadeh was told that she had to return to Afghanistan with her mother. There was a man waiting for her at home.

Preparations for a son's marriage included raising money to purchase the bride, and to do that, Alizadeh's mother had decided to sell her daughter into marriage first. Her brother needed $7000 as dowry for his soon-to-be bride. Alizadeh would be sold for $9000.

Alizadeh's is the story of as many as 12 million girls in Afghanistan who are married off as children every year, all for the tradition of a bride price. In fact, Alizadeh's family had sold her into forced marriage at the early age of ten once. Luckily for her, the contract fell through then. The second time around, however, Alizadeh did not want to leave it to luck. She decided to rebel in the way she knew best—by writing and recording a rap song.

When Alizadeh had first heard Eminem rap, something about the beat and the urgency in his voice had enthralled her. She couldn't understand the words, but she was hooked. Having developed an interest in music through videos she saw on the television, she started writing pop songs but soon realized she had 'too much to say' and switched to rap, with her favourites— Iranian rapper Yas and Eminem—guiding her pace and style.

As a female, singing solo without special permission from the Iranian government is illegal. So Alizadeh rapped in secret, with the help of a few rebellious music producers, about the war in Afghanistan and the challenges she faced as a refugee, a child labourer and a woman. But she did catch the attention of documentary film-maker Rokhsareh Ghaemmaghami, who decided to film the beautiful but dispirited Alizadeh. She even paid her mother $2000 to let her daughter stay in Iran.

Alizadeh's rap song, 'Brides for Sale' went viral, with over 1.4 million views to date!

'Let me whisper to you my words
So no one hears that I speak of the selling of girls.
My voice shouldn't be heard as it is against sharia
Women must remain silent. This is this city's tradition.
I scream to make up for a woman's lifetime silence
I scream on behalf of the deep wounds on my body.
I scream for a body exhausted in its cage
A body that broke under the price tags you put on it.'

The white wedding dress against the black background, her distressed face painted with bleeding wounds and a barcode across her forehead were all grotesque reminders of her child-bride fate as she rapped so that she could be seen as more than a price tag.

A few weeks later, the Strongheart Group, an organization that helps individuals directly impacted by social issues, heard her plea and offered to sponsor a student visa for her to come to the United States and a full scholarship to see her through high school.

Alizadeh did not hesitate to take the offer. And although it took her a few months to tell her mother where she was, her family began encouraging her music after she sent them money following her first concert in the US in May. But more importantly, her family stopped pressurizing her and her sister into marriage, and her voice made all the difference.

Alizadeh's biggest fear is to see a world where girls continue to be treated as property, unable to imagine or create a bright future for themselves, and to see world leaders not take action to end gender-based violence around the world.

She ultimately wants to return to Afghanistan, pay the kindness that Ghaemmaghami showed her forward and fight for women's rights through her rap. The petite girl, her long dark hair and big eyes shining with a determination to make this happen, understands the danger of being a female activist in her conservative country. But she believes her country and the cause need her because if she can change her family's mind with her music, she can change the whole world with it.

And she is inspiring real change, given that hers is one of the many heroic stories featured in the bestselling book, *Goodnight Stories for Rebel Girls*. For now, she continues to write and rap, hoping her voice reaches more girls who need the courage to speak up.

BREATHING

Dhayana Alejandrina
(Dominican Republic/United States)

Today it is easier to breathe.
My heart no longer carries
the heavy weights from the past.
I am filling my lungs with kindness,
forgiveness, and sincerity.

* Curated by *The Alipore Post*

34

Education for All

AN INITIATIVE TO BRING DIGITAL LEARNING TO EVERYONE

Fiji

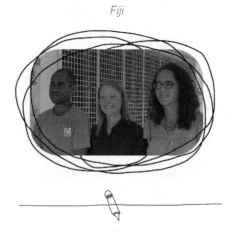

When the pandemic shut down schools around the world, leaving many children in low-resource and unconnected communities across Africa with no learning materials, the non-profit Empower Kids South Sudan got to work to change that. They started training facilitators to bring SolarSPELL devices to Juba, South Sudan, so students could access its free digital resources.

Designed specifically for underserved communities like the ones in Juba, the SolarSPELL is a digital library that generates its own Wi-Fi hotspot, enabling anyone with a device to freely surf the library's expansive and localized content without the need for the internet or electricity. The device, designed and produced by Arizona State University students and professors, empowers students with twenty-first century teaching and learning materials without the need for costly, long-term infrastructure.

In Juba, where the project 'Implementation of Distance Learning Program through Digital Library' ran from July to October 2020, a total of 1,25,674 textbooks and other educational resources were downloaded from SolarSPELL digital libraries, and 35,262 primary and secondary students and fifty-four primary and secondary schools gained access to textbooks and other resources.

Yet the library by itself is not empowering. The technology needs to be matched with teachers who are committed to locate relevant resources, incorporate them in their teaching and also train students in internet-ready skills. Like Master Orisi, a passionate teacher at Navakawau Primary in the Navakawau Village on Taveuni Island, Fiji. In his nineteen years of working as a teacher, Orisi has always looked for ways to improvise his teaching methods to make up for the sheer lack of resources like textbooks, internet, electricity and more in his village. So when, in 2018, the SolarSPELL offline digital library was introduced in schools across Fiji, including Orisi's, no one was happier than him.

'Once I was equipped with advanced educational resources, I was inspired to go above and beyond my normal efforts,' says Orisi, who started using interactive visual aids for topics such as climate change, maths and English; expanding on applicable activities for each lesson and offering his students extra review classes in the evenings, after working hours.

Later that same school year, Orisi's eighth grade students received the best national end-of-year exam results they'd ever recorded, and all continued on to secondary school.

Similar is the story of other schools in Fiji, like Vunisaiki Primary School, Uluivalili College, Vunidawa Primary, St. Mary's Primary, Korokadi Primary and Natewa District School.

But what makes SolarSPELL a real success is not simply the equality of access but also the carefully curated knowledge that is localized and relevant. SolarSPELL's implantation plan includes visits to field sites to monitor impact. Through tools such as usage tracking software, surveys and interviews, they gather feedback that then facilitates improvements in libraries, hardware, software, trainings and product implementations.

'Learning takes place when the thing you're learning can be recognizable—when you can relate to it and understand it as your own,' says Laura Hosman, co-founder and director at SolarSPELL.

During her visit to Taveuni, where she met Orisi and his countless students, she reports that the children's faces lit up when they watched new videos, learnt how to add large numbers on a new app SolarSPELL is developing, and read stories they could truly recognize.

Working on the values of building a world community, learning and bridging the gap in quality education, SolarSPELL currently has 365 digital libraries in Fiji, Vanuatu, Samoa, Tonga, the Federated States of Micronesia, Rwanda, South Sudan and Comoros, with plans to implement 500 and more libraries and expand to Latin America and across East Africa.

'When I first came to this school three years ago, it had been scoring 29 per cent for the overall external exams.

The second year we managed to move it up to 54 per cent. But last year we got 100 per cent,' says another eighth grade teacher in the Natewa District School. 'Thanks to the SolarSPELL, my children have access to the world.'

The greatest
impact of an
act of kindness
is felt on
the self

35
One Man's Trash . . .

SANITATION WORKERS RESCUE
BOOKS FROM THE GARBAGE

Turkey

Every morning, no matter the weather, a group of sanitation workers in the city of Ankara, Turkey, get to their job of emptying every garbage can in the capital city, making sure to rummage through each bag carefully to look for books.

The ones found are inspected, cleaned, sorted and stamped before they make their way on to the shelves of the library they've set up.

'As a child, I would have loved to have books. But we lived in a poor district, and there weren't many schoolbooks on sale, not that we could afford them,' says Güven Akin, a garbage collector and one of the book rescuers. The library has given them all a chance to find books they like and educate themselves. There is something for everyone, they say.

It all started when Dursun Ipek found bags of books thrown away next to the trash cans while on duty. After a quick consultation with their director, Ipek and some colleagues, who did not believe that books belonged in the trash, decided to give a second lease of life to those destined for the landfills. They started taking the books back home or giving them to kids around.

As their collection grew, they found a new home for it in the vacant brick factory on the premises of the sanitation department's headquarters in the Çankaya district. Soon the public started to take more interest, with a flurry of books being donated straight to them. What was initially a library available only to sanitation employees and their families, opened its doors to the public in December 2017. The municipality has also hired a full-time employee to manage the library.

Over the last ten years, the number of bookworms in Turkey has risen from 30 to 42 per cent, and the library is part of this growing trend.

'Village schoolteachers from all over Turkey are requesting books,' says Çankaya's mayor Alper Taşdelen, whose local government oversaw the opening of the library. To address this need, the group plans to convert a garbage truck into a mobile library to reach village schools.

There is only one regret that the team has—that they didn't start sooner.

Nevertheless, they continue to work towards growing the library and turning trash into treasure. In fact, they are also budding musicians who found their instruments doing their daily garbage collection rounds.

'There is always such a nice, hollow sound when you beat on the empty cans!' Akin says with a smile. He is part of the garbage orchestra that is hoping to perform abroad one day.

ele

* This story was adapted from an article originally published on Goodnet.org, a kindness collaborator of UNESCO MGIEP.

36

Fight Face

**A WOMAN TRAINS OTHERS
TO FIGHT BACK**

Jordan

'I'm a troublemaker,' Lina Khalifeh says, introducing herself by the title her father gave her for all the trouble she was up to as a young girl. She fought with boys to prove she was stronger and smarter than them, got bullied by them for it, and yet also punished by her parents thereafter. But, despite it all, she kept going back to fight again the next day.

That's because Khalifeh believed she was born to fight. It is what god and life wanted her to do.

She began with taekwondo at the age of five and was on her way to a successful career as a professional fighter. But her dreams were put on hold when she injured her knee in a fight (which she adds did win her the gold!).

It was while recovering from this injury that she noticed that her friend Sara had bruises all over her face. Upon prodding, Sara told Khalifeh that she was being beaten up by her brother and father, but refused to take help or do anything about it.

'This made me so angry,' recalls Khalifeh, who decided right then that she was going to start teaching self-defence.

In Jordan, where Khalifeh has been born and brought up, UN statistics from 2013 show that almost a quarter of girls and women, aged 15–49, experience physical or sexual violence in their lifetime. About 14 per cent had been abused in the previous twelve months.

While the country has laws against domestic violence, the definition of violence under them is unclear and often favours reconciliation over asylum for the abused. The law also doesn't view rape within marriage as a crime.

Khalifeh began training a few girls in the basement of her parents' home. A year later, she partnered with local gyms to host her class there, but before long she set up her own self-defence studio because of the increasing demand.

That is how SheFighter, the first and only female self-defence studio in the Middle East, was born in 2012 in Amman.

Of course, it wasn't all that simple. 'First, you're a woman. Second, you're a woman in business. Third, you're starting something that is really new to the whole society.' What she did wasn't always met with kindness. Khalifeh found herself fighting against many who believed that women would neither be able to nor should they defend themselves, and her idea would fail.

One of her student's husband even sued her for teaching his wife self-defence, which she used against him when he tried to beat her!

Over the years, SheFighter has trained more than 25,000 women globally and certified over 700 instructors till date in the SheFighter system in thirty-five countries. They've found themselves training in schools, universities and NGOs, channelling kindness as they empower women to fight violence and find their voice. SheFighter now has twelve trainers giving lessons in taekwondo, boxing, kung fu, regular boxing as well as counselling, and is working to open more locations in Saudi Arabia and Kuwait.

'SheFighter has changed my life,' explains Batoul Jaikat, one of the instructors who has been trained by Khalifeh, 'not just physically, but also psychologically. Here in Jordan, most of the girls wait for someone to help them, but here at SheFighter, we're trying to change this.'

And the change is evident in the women they train. Take Lubna, for example. After three years of training at SheFighter, Lubna was attacked by a stranger who pushed her into an elevator and tried to rape her. Her first response was fear, but she quickly found her power and began fighting back until the man gave up and ran away. But with the help of a few people on the street, she not only caught him but also roughed him up. The man ended up in jail.

'Attackers are cowards,' says Khalifeh with a laugh, recalling an incident with another SheFighter trainee who was returning home at night when she was followed by a man who caught up with her and put his hand on her shoulder. 'All it took was her turning around and putting on a fighting stance for him to run away!'

These stories, the many awards and the recognition she has received keep her going and so does a quote by Madeleine Albright she has put up around her studio to remind her of her purpose: 'It took me a long time to develop a voice, but now that I have one, I'm not going to be silent'.

37

Fashioning Change

**A YOUNG BOY'S DRIVE TO CREATE
AWARENESS THROUGH FASHION**

Hong Kong

Aaron Lit was four when he first went snorkelling and ten when he took his first scuba-dive, a camera in hand, to make sure he captured the experience for his mother and friends back home.

The years that followed were scattered with innumerable scuba dives. With the growing passion for scuba diving inherited from his father and his personal intrigue for the beauty of marine biodiversity, Lit's simple photography transformed into an art form, some of which would get published soon after.

As Lit grew older, he learnt how drastic an impact our lifestyles have on the smaller sea creatures, many almost unknown to us, more than the larger ones; how all the conservation efforts are targeted towards dolphins, whales and turtles; and how there's a huge oversight in terms of what we have to do in order to sustain the bottom of the food chain.

Lit wanted to find more artistic ways to represent marine biodiversity beyond his photographs. Thanks to his mother, who is a fashion designer back home in Hong Kong, he found fabric. He learnt that simple acts like washing polyester clothing in washing machines produced millions of beads of microfibres that proved deadly to smaller marine creatures. That everyday habits like using plastic that is destined to live in the ocean for hundreds of years destroys the digestive system of animals. And that the fashion industry was one of the largest polluters in the world.

An environmentally engaged fashion line, with sustainable production methods and plant-based fibres, was a perfect way to capture the diversity of colours, patterns and textures of the underwater world, while promoting marine biodiversity conservation.

That is how MiaMira was born, with the aim to create a bridge between the creatures that inspire the garments and the people wearing them. It was his way of raising awareness about the damages that current patterns of production and consumerism in the world of fashion cause and hopes that his work feeds into the efforts to protect life underwater, which is the fourteenth goal in the SDGs. Lit believes that egoism fuels anti-SDG action. Whether it's prioritizing self-interests or profits at the expense of a community or even an ecosystem, egoistic actions make one see themselves as the only means and others as an end to their means. Instead, he hopes that people turn to kindness.

Kindness, Lit believes, makes you spare a thought for others. One sacrifices their time, convenience and profits so that someone else benefits and, more importantly, is not negatively impacted. He believes that that is what SDGs are all about.

Lit is currently battling the high costs of sustainable fashion to achieve his goal to reinvent the supply chain, all the while making sure to also give back directly to the marine life. Currently, all profits go to the Hong Kong Aquatic Life Conservation Fund that sponsors field trips for students from underprivileged backgrounds to educate them about marine conservation.

38

Glow Heartfulness Webinars

**HELPING WOMEN AROUND THE
GLOBE BE KIND TO THEMSELVES**

United States

On the day Sophia Neghesti Johnson was prescribed antidepressants, she decided to attend a meditation session instead. She was hesitant to start on medication and wanted to see if she could find help in some other way.

This is a positive story, so we already know that it worked, but that it would be a roaring success was not something Neghesti had expected. The first session helped her so much that she continued to attend more weekly sessions and went on to arrange for regular personal meditation sessions with the trainer too. She soon realized that she had completely forgotten about her medication for depression!

Neghesti was part of the World Moms Network, a media organization in the United States. She was among the handful of women who first attended the online Heartfulness meditation sessions in 2015 organized by the Heartfulness Institute. This was an initiative to impart heart-based relaxation and meditation through online webinars with the aim to cleanse the mind, rejuvenate and refresh and connect with oneself.

After a year of attending these webinars and seeing a shift in her relationship with herself, Neghesti joined a couple of women to become a trainer herself and help more women. The experience also led the Heartfulness meditation trainers to identify a need to include more women in the Heartfulness project, and so, GLOW (Genuine Loving Outstanding Women) was born.

GLOW is an exclusive webinar series for women that is designed to provide solutions for the many challenges that women face and support balance and harmony in the myriad roles that women play in today's society, all with the heart at its centre. The heart is where solutions are birthed, where joy and love and light exist, and when the heart is purified and balanced, creative opportunities are recognized. This is the balance that GLOW aims to achieve.

The webinars, led by women speakers who are experts in their chosen fields, offer a space to share perspectives and loving guidance to help make the personal and professional lives of women joyful and purposeful. They span discussions on health, well-being, inspiration, guidance, leadership, parenting and family tips, all with the power of the Heartfulness meditation at the core, which forms the basis of a loving, kind and compassionate approach towards finding solutions.

Imagine a young girl from rural India speaking to a Miss World beauty pageant winner, a young entrepreneur from a middle-class family in Portugal speaking to CEOs of Fortune 500 companies, or an adolescent who is differently abled in Guatemala asking the UNESCO chair researcher about opportunities to play sports.

Thanks to GLOW, this is not left to the imagination and instead has been experienced in the webinars that have over 1 million views to date.

'GLOW's online presence has opened its practices and knowledge to those who wish to experience the practice from the comfort of their own home, at their workplace or in communities and neighbourhoods,' says Nancy Sumari, executive director of The Neghesti-Sumari Foundation and Miss Tanzania and Miss World Africa 2005.

And they've been doing all this while contributing to achieving certain SDGs of the UN like good health and well-being, gender equality, quality education, and decent work and economic growth.

'The GLOW webinar series is innovative in that it brings the heart and aspect of inner work to global issues. It has been scaled for global reach through the actively engaged online network and therefore has a high impact,' says Aisling Clardy (formerly Sugrue), UNESCO chair researcher.

GLOW believes that the greatest impact of an act of kindness is felt on the self and that engaging in regular acts of kindness is the way to heal and alter oneself while finding solutions to problems big and small. How great of an impact would we then see if women, who are often burdened by responsibilities and expectations, learn to be kind to themselves? The team of 14,000 trainers strive for just this impact with every mediation and discussion session.

* This story was adapted from an article originally published by The Heartfulness Institute, a kindness collaborator of UNESCO MGIEP.

39

Education for All

**AN INTERVIEW WITH
TANIA ROSAS**

Colombia

'We aim to democratize quality education,' says Tania. The twenty-nine-year-old political scientist and educational researcher from La Guajira, Colombia, is working to achieve that through her organization Origin Learning Fund (Fundación El Origen)—an NGO that facilitates access to personalized digital education for underrepresented communities, which have encountered a large gap in information technology and quality education—and her latest learning app, O-lab.

You say you've seen an unjust world ever since you were a child.

La Guajira has been the nest of epidemics such as drug trafficking, smuggling, illegal armed groups, child recruitment, pollution, overexploitation of natural resources and corruption amongst many other abuses. Thousands of children and young people grow up without dreams of being and doing great because all they've seen are unhappy marriages, malnutrition, sexual abuse, unworthy jobs and poverty.

I went to one of the largest public schools for girls in La Guajira where quality personalized education was not possible, but having parents who were first-generation college graduates and also being able to access a computer at home for what I had not understood in class, helped me to continue and further my education. But this was a privilege since most of the students in my school didn't have that kind of support, still, today many of the students in my region are lacking support to thrive, that is why despite state efforts, La Guajira has the highest school dropouts, illiteracy and poverty rates in the country generation over generation.

Can you tell us about your inspiration behind Origin Learning Fund?

Origin Learning Fund is a coming together of stories from people inspired by the idea of changing the future of young people at risk. My grandmother Rosa 'Ocha' founded a school in her home to provide personalized, inclusive and empowering education to young people who were being excluded from regular schools.

She died when I was thirteen years old. She has been my biggest inspiration and continues to be my driving force for OLF.

Why do you think access to learning opportunities is the best way to sustainable development?

Everything starts with education. The data I collected from the communities showed that those who could further their education were more likely to overcome poverty. More specifically, in indigenous communities, when a young woman is out of school, it affects whole communities and translates to gender violence, forced marriages and teenage pregnancies.

So, I decided to focus on how we can improve access to reliable, inclusive, personalized, accessible and quality twenty-first-century education in underrepresented communities with poor connectivity, youth in at-risk situations and a serious lack of trained teachers.

Today, the majority of people across the developing world now have access to a mobile phone. Access to mobile means access to information, and access to information means having the ability to make sustainable livelihoods. That is why we focused on developing a personalized mobile solution for local schools and organizations to provide a personalized education that guides young people to become leaders capable to overcome poverty and build sustainable communities.

We have come together as a group with the most underrepresented communities, working with partner organizations and institutions to develop education methodologies and designs, testing every step of our solution and respond quickly to their feedback.

Results show that 8 out of 10 beneficiaries further their education (6–17-year-olds), 8 out of 10 got certified in at least one complementary course (13–28-year-olds) and 5 out of 10 began a STEAM or entrepreneurship project (16–28-year-olds). We also saw young women who completed our entrepreneurship courses go on to create employment opportunities in their own community!

After O-lab, the count has reached 50,000 young people. How did the idea of O-lab come about?

The idea of O-Lab came after many years of research when I founded Fundación El Origen in Colombia back in 2015 and then in the United States as Origin Learning Fund. O-lab is a learning management system (LMS) with an app that works both online and offline and in low-cost devices. It includes a virtual tutor that is adapted to each community and their local language (even indigenous tongues), and contains high-quality content created by partner organizations, corporates and educational institutions worldwide. We train local teachers and leaders to implement O-lab that along with our analytics platform, which produces clear results on learners' progress, allows schools and governments to improve their pedagogical approach and quality education based on real-time data.

Here I would also like to thank my partner Rene, who helped me shape my vision and my great team of young innovators that makes it possible.

You have now launched the Origin Learning Fund in the United States. What is next for Origin Learning Fund?

By 2020, when the pandemic forced school closures worldwide, students were dropping out of school because of the lack of access to digital education. More than 11 million girls around the world could not return to school after the Covid-19 crisis. So I immediately decided to reach out to organizations worldwide and asked them to try O-lab. And they loved it. In fact, it allowed them to continue their educational projects and it also helped schools bring students back. Today, a growing number of organizations, foundations, institutions and leaders across the world are using O-lab to ensure access to digital education for all.

Fighting low resources, but driven by kindness and a lot of passion, Tania and her team have been able to grow a solution that leaves no one behind and are now working on developing a more comprehensive and scalable approach that can be adaptable to any culture, language and context worldwide.

40
A New Lease of Life

**A SHELTER WORKING TO GIVE OUR CANINE
FRIENDS A SECOND CHANCE AT LIFE**

Romania

Bucur spends most of his days playing in the grass, being tended to by his physiotherapist and living the most joyful life possible. But this wasn't the Bucur the folks at Adăpostul Speranța had first encountered. When he had been picked up from a wasteland near Bucharest, badly injured, he had everyone worried because of his cries and shivers. Not only was he paraplegic, which had left him crawling on the ground, he was also extremely malnourished. But with a little bit of love, a specially-tailored dog wheelchair, regular physiotherapy, Bucur, whose name means 'joy' in Romanian, began to thrive.

This is what Adăpostul Speranța has done for so many paraplegic canines around the city.

Adăpostul Speranța was created in 2001, in the heat of the moment, when Traian Băsescu, Bucharest's mayor at the time, ordered that all stray dogs be killed. Founded by Florina Tomescu, thousands of animals were saved and adopted due to her involvement and perseverance. She is the reason for the success of the foundation. The shelter's first mission was a mass rescue on the night of 18 April 2001. The staff of Speranța Foundation and other partner organizations, such as VIER PFOTEN, an organization based in Vienna, who are their sponsors and now friends for almost twenty years, rescued 300 dogs from the city hall's shelters that night, dogs that would have been otherwise euthanized under the new law. As of 2021, twenty of these veterans are still living a happy life in the shelter, as did most of the others until the end of their lives.

The organization's motto is to leave no dog behind. They refuse to end a life that they believe, with proper care, can be a happy one.

The shelter refuses to put a dog to sleep unless in the worst of cases, when it could save them from a life of torment and pain. Therefore, it has taken the responsibility of caring for injured and paraplegic dogs, not only by providing them a safe home but also wheels, so they can lead a normal life of adventure and curiosity.

Similar to Bucur's is the case of another dog who was hit by a car in Vaslui, a small city in eastern Romania. The person who accidentally hit the dog, brought him to Speranța where he was diagnosed with two broken legs and operated on twice to insert two rods and a metal plate. The team is certain that with love and care, he is sure to be able to walk again.

Such work is hard, financially draining and only possible with the kindness of volunteers and donors. Unfortunately, as the dogs get bigger, they need new carts. Then there are those that have broken or simply worn out from all the activity that the dogs are up to. Most recently, the shelter put up a social media post asking for donations for eleven carts they desperately need.

But despite all the challenges, there's no stopping the team from spreading their kindness to our canine friends.

The happiness of the paraplegic dogs is the team's reward. And one can only imagine the smiles that these animals can bring as they skitter around on their wheels, enjoying the sun and the grass like all other dogs.

PUPPY'S HEART

Juansen Dizon
(Manila)

kindness
makes
the soft strong
and the strong soft

* Curated by *The Alipore Post*

41

The Ones That Walked with Mammoths

**A YOUNG CONSERVATIONIST
WORKING TO SAVE THE ANTELOPES**

Uzbekistan

Their big black and bulgy eyes, long wriggly funnel-like noses, striped pinkish-yellow horns and 70 kmph whizzing legs may make one think of the saiga antelope as creatures from a work of science fiction and not as mammals who've been around since the ice age, outliving mammoths and sabre-toothed tigers. Having migrated across arid plains in Eastern Europe, Asia and Alaska, the saiga antelopes are now found in Kazakhstan, Mongolia, Russia, Turkmenistan and Uzbekistan, where Olya Esipova, one of the leading saiga antelope conservationists, is from.

Born to a family of dedicated biologists, Esipova's love and kind outlook towards wildlife and nature was ingrained in her at a very young age. 'I would travel with my parents to the most amazing wildlife locations, and I remember this one time when I saw herds of saigas migrating from south to north to find better pastures,' recalls Esipova.

This was her first encounter with the saiga antelope. Esipova soon learnt that saiga populations had been dramatically declining for years. Larger discussions with her parents and literature on conservation all pointed to the fact that there was a need to affect behavioural changes to protect wildlife.

This led her to take the first step to wildlife conservation, with one animal close to home that needed help. Her plan of action was to study psychology so that she could work with local communities to help change their attitude and actions towards the saiga.

'This decline is occurring in a country like Uzbekistan, where the local culture talks about the saiga in their folk tales and traditional crafts and it is believed to be a magical animal that brings luck!' exclaims Esipova.

In the 1980s, their population was over a million. Then came the collapse of the Soviet Union, which brought with it desperate times. People lost their jobs and ended up in total poverty, picking up any means of income they could find, including poaching saigas, bringing down their count by 95 per cent to only 50,000.

Thankfully, successful conservation efforts brought the population back to a quarter of a million, until 2015. Climate change and an increase in temperature by 10 degrees led to mass deaths of the mammal due to a bacterial infection. And 60 per cent of the population was wiped out once again.

'For us, it was a massive wake-up call that there was a chance that the saiga were vulnerable . . . and it was something we could not control,' Esipova says, a resolve in her eyes.

The next best step would be to limit the threats to the saiga population that they could control. These included hunting for their meat and valuable horns, keeping a check on oil and gas exploration and transportation, laying of new road and rail infrastructures that hindered saiga migrations and monitoring an increase in livestock numbers to avoid impeding access to traditional pastures that the antelopes need to feed on. She worked with people to inspire them to participate in lasting conservation efforts and helped them understand the value of nature for long-term climate control. This was the only way the young conservationist believed all of the issues could be corrected.

A simple example of such an awareness and conservation drive that Esipova led with her team at the Saiga Conservation Alliance (SCA)—a network of researchers and conservationists who have been studying and protecting the critically endangered prehistoric saiga antelope for over fifteen years—was a mural project in a local school where they worked to paint a wildlife wall. She started with three volunteers and finished with children fighting for space in the wall to paint an animal of their choice, all leaving with the understanding of the importance of wildlife conservation.

And there have been many wins in the conservation journey for the people of Uzbekistan. Like the development of 'the saiga transects census method' that allows the conservationists to collect data on the saiga population in the Ustyurt Plateau in Uzbekistan, training of rangers for dedicated saiga conservation and officers working with law enforcement agencies on illegal trade, and social education events such as the Day of Protected Areas and the Saiga Day.

In her personal journey as a field zoologist and conservationist, too, Esipova has grown leaps and bounds since being a volunteer as a teenager. From winning the Young Conservation Leadership Award in 2014 and being selected to intern with three leading wildlife organizations in Kenya to founding Youth for Wildlife Conservation and rising through the ranks to become the Research and Development Officer of SCA's Uzbekistan programme—the young girl is unstoppable. Currently, she is finishing her internship with the International Sustainability Academy in Germany and is conducting research in Uzbekistan's Aral Sea region. And there is lots more to come, including starting a dream school for environmental studies!

'Climate change, global warming, habitat close, deforestation . . . We hear all these terms and are lost. We don't know what to do, where to start, why to care. So we tend to ignore it. But if you think about what to do, let's make it simple—let's take one species and one problem and one action towards finding a solution for it,' she concludes.

42

Out with the Old

A YOUNG MAN'S DREAM TO LIGHT UP THE LIVES OF OTHERS

Philippines

'As a kid—and I was a cute kid—' Mark Lozano smiles shyly before continuing, 'I thought my only responsibility was to study and get high grades . . . I never pushed to help people, bring change . . . because I was told I was too young . . . that I should wait until I get a job.'

For Lozano, who went on to start One Million Lights Philippines (OML PH), this mindset changed when his school nominated him to attend an international youth conference at the age of sixteen. Mark knew then that this was an opportunity to expand his perspective of his world and he met teenagers as young as himself working on large-scale development projects.

Lozano recognized that being young did not have to prevent someone from helping others and so, he immediately decided to find a way to transform the world. He enlisted his friend Trisha to help and the two began researching on how they could help communities back home in the Philippines.

When they came across the California-based non-profit One Million Lights, which works towards replacing toxic, hazardous and costly kerosene lamps with clean, safe and affordable solar-powered lights, a light bulb (solar-powered in this case!) went off in their heads.

Almost 2.3 million families consisting of 132 million Filipinos live in isolated communities throughout the country with no access to basic infrastructure, including electricity, for which they rely on kerosene. The numbers were greater in 2010, when Lozano began. Research shows that four hours of exposure to kerosene fumes every night is equivalent to smoking two packs of cigarettes. It is also one of the leading causes of house fires. Health risks aside, the most pertinent problem for these communities is the cost of kerosene itself, which eats up to 30 per cent of their monthly income.

This was how they would bring about change, by founding the Philippines chapter of One Million Lights.

Lozano and Trisha chose to begin with Barangay Dugui Too, an isolated community in Catanduanes, a small island mountain in the south of the Philippines. The community lives in an area that is in the path of some of the strongest typhoons that hit the Philippines, which means that their houses are destroyed and they have to relocate annually, and electricity isn't even an option because it is not economical for the electric companies to extend lines there.

OML PH decided to distribute 200 solar-powered lights to all the 200 families that were part of Barangay Dugui Too.

With no knowledge but heaps of zeal, the two got to work. They raised funds and sourced lights, although everything that could go wrong did in the next seven months.

Fundraising was difficult. Almost everyone they met thought that they were too young to be trusted. 'Someone even asked if I had especially bought a shirt for the meeting!' recalls Lozano. When they did raise funds through campaigns in the United States, Canada and South Africa, their supplier in the US went bankrupt. And when they found a factory in China that was making the lights, the airline that their shipment was being transported on went on strike, with their lights getting stuck in customs.

But the two had made a promise to the community that they would be back with the solar-powered lights and so, they continued to struggle to find solutions. Thanks to the kindness of a customs broker who helped release their shipment, which arrived at the island via bus and then ferry a day before they were meant to start their project.

'Just hearing them say *mabalos!* ("thank you" in Bicolano) made everything worth it,' says Lozano, with determination in his voice.

'I look at kindness as a bridge to acting with empathy. It is what fuels the drive for me to work on these initiatives and allows me to be more open to the people I am working with.'

Since kick-starting the initiative, OML PH has helped light up forty out of eighty-one provinces in the Philippines, providing over 22,364 families with access to solar lighting. But Lozano says he has a long way to go before he hits the one million mark.

43
Women in the Lead

THE YOUNGEST MINISTER
OF TUNISIA

Tunisia

When Saida Ounissi returned to Tunisia for the first time, she could never have anticipated that her path would become intimately linked to the country's fate. When she was five, her family was forced to exile when the country was buckling under the dictatorship of former President Ben Ali. They would see the country again twenty years later, after the collapse of the regime in 2011.

Although suffering the consequences of dictatorship all along their exile, their parents were keen to transmit their ideals to their children, bringing them along to peace protests and meetings, showing them documentaries and reading newspapers together.

Making them socially conscious from a very young age, they strongly believed that awareness was the first step towards action. Leading by example, they naturally encouraged their children to show generosity and compassion by involving them in their social actions towards newly arrived refugees in France.

Ounissi's political awakening was consolidated during her student years when she enrolled for masters in political sciences and development studies in Sorbonne Université. She was very active in the civil society, involved in European Students' Union and intercultural dialogue initiatives to foster understanding between young people from different religious and social backgrounds.

She was still very vocal about her political beliefs when she arrived in Tunis after the revolution to work for the African Development Bank. Soon enough, Ounissi became one of the most relevant young voices in Tunisia, drawing attention from international organizations, which frequently invited her to share her analysis about the democratization process following the Arab Spring.

While working as a political analyst and pursuing a PhD in social policies, she was invited by Ennahda Party to invigorate the vision of a movement that historically opposed authoritarianism for the past forty years.

At twenty-seven, she was elected Member of Parliament. Two years later, she was appointed as Secretary of State in charge of vocational training. In 2018, she was finally nominated in the Ministry of Employment, making her the youngest minister in Tunisia's political history.

Today, Tunisia is leading the way for women's rights. The last ten years saw a significant shift, with 23 per cent of ministers and 19.5 per cent of the new government made up of women. Currently, women account for over 35 per cent of the country's MPs, making it one of the top 30 in the world. In fact, since the Arab Spring, the country has been a catalyst for women participation. Their voices have been crucial during the drafting process of the new constitution and reforming electoral laws. In fact, in every aspect of the transition to democracy, women have driven progressive policies, and Ounissi follows in this legacy. As a political leader in Tunisia and a member of the Muslim democrats party Ennahda, she has been at the forefront of pushing for gender parity, forbidding human trafficking and forced labour. She played a pivotal role in overseeing the first-ever legislation aimed at tackling violence against women.

'The state is now being pushed to acknowledge that even if you are violent towards women behind closed doors, you must be held accountable to the rest of society,' says Ounissi. Furthermore, she has subsequently helped implement the revolutionary Startup Act, which encourages technological innovation and the development of small businesses that are generally female-owned. Indeed, Ounissi believes that financial autonomy is one way to achieve gender equality.

But the journey of being a decision maker in a burgeoning democracy has not been easy. Ounissi had to earn her place as a young woman showing initiative within an ageing political class, which tends to dismiss the younger generation.

Nonetheless, growing up in a family where spirituality always had a central place, she can count on a solid support system. Together, they pray to bring her peace and moral strength in troubled times. When she is off duty, she always makes sure to spend time with her loved ones to overcome her daily battles and find inspiration. She values empathy over everything else and embodies the principles transmitted by her family by rooting her actions in a larger path that exceeds her personal views, always favouring the global well-being over her own interest.

She took as a personal vocation the challenge to restore trust between the citizens and their public institutions. She is endlessly working for reconciliation within a national community shattered by decades of tyranny, pushing for a genuine democratic dialogue to build a truly resilient society.

44

United by Religion

A CHURCH OPENS ITS DOOR FOR RAMADAN DINNERS

Spain

'All things therefore whatsoever ye would that men should do to you, do ye even so to them: for this is the law and the prophets.'

—Bible, St Matthew

Almost every religion in the globe has its own version of the golden rule that tells them to treat others as they want to be treated.

A Catholic leader offering a safe space for Muslims to gather and break their fast during Ramadan is a prime example of the golden rule in action—in this case, treating the other with the same kindness you would hope for yourself.

'People are very happy that Muslims can do Iftar in a Catholic church, because religions serve to unite us, not to separate us,' says Faouzia Chati, the president of the Catalan Association of Moroccan Women.

One of the five Pillars of Islam, Ramadan is one of the holiest Islamic months during which observant Muslims do not eat between sunrise and sunset, and break their fast only at nightfall at the evening meal called Iftar. It is a time when Muslims are encouraged to give to charity, pray to strengthen their connect with God, and show kindness and patience.

In Barcelona, Chati used to organize Iftar gatherings across the city, but with the Covid-19 pandemic enforcing a limit on indoor dining, she was forced to look for an alternative open space with room for distancing.

Fortunately, Father Peio Sanchez, Santa Ana's rector, who sees the coming together of different faiths as a symbol of civic coexistence, offered his assistance. 'Even with different cultures, different languages, different religions, we are more capable of sitting down and talking than some politicians,' he says. He opened the doors of the Catholic church's open-air cloisters to local Muslims for Iftar.

To add to the community spirit, volunteers gathered to serve free home-cooked Iftar meals to 50–60 Muslims, many of them homeless, in the century-old stone passages of Santa Ana Church.

Another story of the golden rule in action is of a Sikh grocery store owner in Pakistan who follows the family tradition of giving special discounts during the holy month. As are the acts of rebuilding a church in the Al Arabi neighbourhood of Mosul, Iraq, by a young group of Muslim volunteers; and a Jewish nurse in Jerusalem breastfeeding a Palestinian baby whose mother was critical after a head-on car collision that killed his father.

Often, we hear religion being used as an excuse for disharmony, but it doesn't have to be.

'As thou deemest thyself so deem others. Then shalt thou become a partner in heaven.'

—Kabir

'We are all the same . . . We are all like brothers and we must help each other too,' says Hafid Oubrahim, a twenty-seven-year-old Moroccan who echoes the community that's been built at the dinners at the Santa Ana Church.

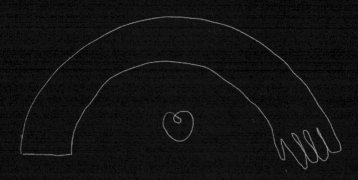

A KINDER WORLD
IS POSSIBLE THROUGH
THE POWER OF

COLLABORATION

Nirmala Mehendale (India), President of the World Kindness Movement

45

A Rose Is a Rose Is a Rose

AN ACTIVIST BATTLING STIGMA, ONE ROSE AT A TIME

Nepal

Sushil Koirala describes himself as the world's biggest dreamer. His dream? To create a more just and peaceful world. And he has been working towards it since 2004, in the midst of the Nepal Civil War.

Koirala was in a medical university in China, far away from his home in the farmlands of the Syangja district in western Nepal, when he grew concerned about the civil conflict in his homeland. He knew he had to do something and that the distance could not be an excuse.

He created a website to campaign against what was happening, posting petitions for peace, publishing articles and writing appeals to garner media attention.

As his commitment to peace began drawing attention, he started public campaigns in and around the university, and soon he received scholarships to attend global youth summits around the world. Koirala took the opportunity to continue spreading his message for peace in Nepal. He collected almost 1000 signatures on his first petition for peace, which he soon presented to the peace minister of Nepal.

By the time Koirala returned home as a doctor, he was more motivated than ever. Peace had become his priority.

In finding innovative ways to spread the message of peace, he started the Rose Movement for World Peace, hoping that instead of guns and war, roses and peace would bring about a revolution in the world.

Why a rose, one may think. Because to Koirala, blooming roses are symbols for children to their full potential, something he hopes to propel through a peaceful environment.

In only two years of its initiation in 2008, rallies of the Rose Movement for World Peace were conducted in Nepal, India, Italy, the Philippines and Switzerland, with over 6000 roses being distributed.

One of the movement's most telling moments was on a sunny afternoon in January 2010, in a rose exchange ceremony at the India–Nepal border. There was mounting strain between the two countries, and instead of sitting and watching, Koirala went into no man's land at the Jamunaha border point, roses in hand. Koirala recalls hundreds of Nepalese and Indian citizens hosting flags, singing anthems and exchanging roses in a gesture of peace and harmony that contributed greatly to calming the tension along the borders.

Fuelled by this success, Koirala, who came to be known as the Rose Doctor, wanted to find other channels for the movement.

So, when on the field, he became involved with the leprosy community and witnessed the difficulties the patients faced on a daily basis, one of them being stigma and discrimination, Koirala expanded his Rose Movement to promote the giving of flowers as a symbol of acceptance and unity along with peace. He began handing out roses to his patients in a gesture of care and oneness.

Understanding that this stigma and prejudice is not only against leprosy but many other diseases, Koirala wants to continue tackling the problem, one rose at a time.

46

The Gift of Sight

AN INTERVIEW WITH
RALF TOENJES

Brazil

For his work in democratizing access to eye care around the world, Ralf Toenjes—founder of the non-profit Renovatio and SDG-led business VerBem—became one of the seventeen UN Young Leaders for the SDGs, selected amongst over 7000 candidates from 172 countries.

We often see seeds of social entrepreneurship being sown in a person at a young age. Can you tell us about growing up in Petrópolis, Brazil?

Not for me, though. What I do today was never on the charts, not even remotely. I had a very ordinary childhood. I went to a great private school, one of the best in the country, and never felt the need for anything. I was nine years old when my parents got divorced. They had a difficult marriage. But my mother supported me through it, as did my teachers, neighbours and friends, which helped build a very nurturing environment.

And you went on to complete three bachelor's degrees in business, economics and law!

It was in university that I first recognized acts of kindness that were meted out to me. The plan was to pursue law (even though maths and physics were my strong suit) because I had seen the respect that my neighbour, who was a judge, received. The motive was to become rich [*laughs*] and be respected, but my father refused to pay for my education, and it was then that the people in my life got together to help me. My mother sold her car, my grandparents helped out, even my high school principal pitched in!

When I recognized this kindness, I did want to do the same for someone else and founded a student organization, Enactus, on my campus. It was when I was travelling to the Enactus World Cup 2013 in Mexico that I came across the statistics around eye care: 680 million people around the world needed glasses but couldn't afford them. In Brazil, 42 million of the population need to wear glasses and don't know. Around 71 per cent of the cities in Brazil don't have an ophthalmologist (and only they can prescribe eyeglasses—no optometrists or similar are allowed in Brazil) and 22.9 per cent of the school dropout rate is due to the lack of proper eye care. Also, I met a German group, OneDollarGlasses, who came up with a solution of affordable eyeglasses. That is when the idea of Renovatio was born and solidified. It was during this time in university that we distributed our first 12,000 glasses in twelve states of Brazil and developed the first Renovatio bus to provide travelling ophthalmologist care in Brazil.

You talk of three reasons that then led you to becoming a social entrepreneur.

Yes, the plan was always to go back to 'regular' work, as society often demands. The first incident that stopped me in my path was something I was told during a leadership course. I was being asked about Renovatio and I explained what we were doing followed by a 'but I'm applying for jobs . . .' One of the leaders immediately asked me why I sounded apologetic for the good work I was doing. This was in December 2015.

A month later, one of my best friends passed away after a short battle with cancer.

The third was the story of Suzanna. A seventy-six-year-old mother of fifteen children and grandmother to fifty-six, Suzanna travelled six hours by boat to our eye camp in Manacapuru to get her eyes tested. And she was able to *see* for the first time in twelve years!

All of these incidents, one after the other, brought me to the understanding of the Renovatio's importance and impact.

How did the idea of VerBam come up?

I recently met a man who, when asked about his eye health, said he used to have glasses but he never got a new pair after they broke. When I asked when that was, he said it was thirty years ago!

Stories like these make me keep going and doing more. With VerBem, which we started in 2017, we have social optical shops where for every pair of glasses sold, we donate up to fourteen pairs of glasses to people who need them.

We began as a team of five and now are a team of forty, and each of us have our own stories of why we do the work we do . . . Each of us do see the change we are creating and the kindness we are receiving and sharing. It all comes together to keep us going.

Since the inception of Renovatio in 2014, Toenjes has set up fifteen travelling ophthalmological clinics, provided eye care to over 2,00,000 people, conducted more than 70,000 eye exams and distributed 60,000 glasses in twenty-three Brazilian states, Mozambique, Haiti and India. 'The reality, when I began, needed kindness, and today it is part of our process, part of the stories we share, whether it is me talking about the people who have helped me or people who talk about me helping them,' Toenjes concludes.

47

After Hours

**A DOCTOR WHO REFUSES TO LET HIS
WORKDAYS DAMPEN HIS PHILANTHROPY**

Malaysia

Studies show that taking time out for philanthropy helps doctors improve their mental health and reduce burnout. Given the commitment that the profession demands, doctors often suffer from feeling disconnected with their work, but volunteer work can make doctors bring back the feeling of fulfilment and motivation.

Dr Ahmad Munawwar Helmi Salim couldn't agree more. 'Being involved in charity work takes me out of the four walls of the hospital. It makes my perspective a more holistic one, so I pay attention to a patient's home condition and emotion too along with their diagnosis,' he says, a toothy smile on his face.

Perhaps this is one reason why he co-founded the Islamic Medical Association of Malaysia's Response and Relief Team (IMARET)—spearheading relief work with the Rohingya refugees, the indigenous people living in rural parts of Malaysia and the sea gypsies on the shores of East Malaysia; establishing of Sekolah Atas Air Hanoverian to provide education for the marginalized children in the shores of Semporna; working with Projek Tongkat to create awareness about amputee football in Malaysia; managing the SafeWhere Initiative that oversees the delivery of safe water to underprivileged communities in Malaysia and to numerous refugee camps around the globe; and assisting frontliners in mass community screening for Covid-19 while raising funds to provide medical supplies to hospitals.

The other reason is because he believes, 'If not us, then who. If not now, then when?' And it is a value of kindness that has been ingrained in him by his family who were always helping someone or with something. It is what came naturally to them, and to Munawwar in turn.

His first 'official' act of charity was in 2011, when he returned to Malaysia after completing his medical degree in Canada, was to raise funds for an orphanage run by a sixty-year-old lady and her son to provide for children with disabilities.

Soon after, he got together with friends at the Islamic Medical Association of Malaysia (IMAM) to organize a futsal charity tournament among the medical fraternity to raise awareness in charity works. Proceeds from the tournament went directly to the orphanage homes.

In 2013, while working under the Ministry of Health, Munawwar was placed in a clinic in a rural part of the east coast of Malaysia. The area, he found out, had earlier been hit by a bad flood, so, once again along with his friends at IMAM, he organized a flood relief to help provide necessary healthcare and food.

On 19 December 2014, the team officially established IMARET, a relief team under IMAM. Only five days later, Malaysia was hit by the worst flood in the history of the nation. Munawwar was given the responsibility to lead the relief effort.

'It was a huge responsibility, but with the support from colleagues and the hundreds of volunteers, IMARET played an essential role in providing medical relief support during the Malaysia East Coast Flood 2014/2015,' recalls Munawwar.

Since then, the initiative has been providing support at almost all annual flood reliefs in the country and assisting at the time of disasters locally and internationally. In fact, in collaboration with other medical NGOs, they have also expanded their relief work to marginalized communities in Malaysia who do not have access to healthcare. Munawwar and his team have made sure that mobile clinics are set up to take care of outpatient care, non-communicable disease treatment, antenatal check-ups, and dental and optometry services.

'We have to make sure that during the non-disaster period, we are expanding the volunteerism and charity work among the medical fraternities,' says Munawwar, when asked about the urgency of his relief work.

And the doctor just keeps on going.

He provides for his two daughters, is the sports doctor at the National Sports Institute of Malaysia and is also pursuing a master's degree in sports medicine. When does he get time to volunteer one may wonder, to which the doctor replies, 'If my "office hours" are 8 a.m. to 5 p.m., the rest of my day I'm a "full-time" volunteer at IMARET.' He goes on to add that he could not do it without his hardworking team and his supportive family that makes it all easy. Of course, this is not to say that the doctor refuses to accept that all the work does get tiring and challenging, but he refuses to rest. 'As long as there are people who need help, we will continue to work. We will only rest when our time in this world is up,' says the kind man, the smile still on his face.

48

Kind-Hearted

**WORKING TO BUILD
A KINDER LANKA**

Sri Lanka

'We have no race, we have no religion, we have no political views. We want to create a movement that inspires everyday people to make a difference in their own way. We know that we might not be able to help every soul in need but we sure will try. We try to work with what we have to get what we need done', reads the Kind Hearted Lankans' manifesto.

And a perfect example of this was the organization's work in the aftermath of the day that has since come to be known as the Easter Bombings.

It was a peaceful Sunday morning on 21 April 2019, when six bombs exploded in three churches and three hotels across Sri Lanka. The blasts claimed 250 lives and left over 500 wounded, as life in Sri Lanka came to a halt. But even before the dust had settled, the team of Kind Hearted Lankans were on the ground, battling bottlenecks they had anticipated at critical emergency facilities like hospitals. Despite the threat of more explosions, the team travelled to hospitals, churches and sites of the explosions to provide critical necessities like clean water, sanitary products and other rations with special permissions from the Sri Lankan government.

Once the immediate needs were met, the team expanded their work to medical aid—helping those with both physical and psychological trauma and supporting those who lost their livelihood.

Kind Hearted Lankans, started in 2015 as one couple's simple endeavour to put aside some of their salary to help a family they knew of, who lived on the side of the roads earning next to nothing selling lottery tickets.

'I did a small video clip of it and it kind of went viral,' says one of the founders of Kind Hearted Lankans who prefers to remain anonymous.

The couple went on to help build a house for the family and there has been no stopping them since. They have been making videos to appeal to the kind side of Lankans to help all those in need. And the support has only been growing.

An early success story that they recall is that of a blind boy who lived in a roadside shack.

'We discovered that this boy could sing very well. We featured him in a video I shared on social media that got people's attention.'

With the help they received, they were able to build a house for him and his family, and he even went on to compete in and win a popular children's singing reality show!

Since then, the team of Kind Hearted Lankans has constructed homes, school buildings and water wells; paid for medical treatments, tuition and the pursuit of dreams; and so much more. Statistics from 2018 say that they have helped over 1000 lives with the backing of kind, like-minded Lankans from around the world, but the team refuses to take credit.

'We have no face, we take no credit, we're simply a movement . . . You won't find any names or logos here. We let the people in our stories be the face of our work. This is not about us, it's about the young mother working dawn till dusk to feed her child and the old man pushing his cart in the sun, wind and rain to make ends meet,' says their vision. And their motto is simple—of kindness, the language which the deaf can hear and the blind can see.

49

Playing for Peace

**A CELLIST FIGHTS TERROR
THROUGH ART**

Iraq

In the aftermath of a devastating explosion, surrounded by rubble, shrapnel and charred remains, Karim Wasfi sets down his chair and leans his cello against himself, closes his eyes and begins to play, his wild locks the only thing about him that fit the unsettled air. And as the tune of the national anthem floods the shopping street in Baghdad's central district of Karrada, which only hours ago had been brought down by a car bomb blast, the voices of passers-by, the police and family and friends of those who had died join in unison to sing along.

A cellist, composer and conductor of the Iraqi National Symphony Orchestra in Baghdad, Wasfi plays amidst the wreckage to defeat ugliness, insanity and terror with beauty, creativity and kindness.

His performance reminds many of the great cellist Mstislav Rostropovich, who brought his instrument to the Berlin Wall and other politically charged venues in an artistic protest against Soviet communism; and the cellist Vedran Smailovic, who became a symbol of artistic opposition to war's destruction when he played in battle-scarred Bosnia.

But this isn't Wasfi's first performance or the one that earns him a place with these musical greats.

Only a week prior to the Karrada blast, an explosion had rocked the neighbourhood of Mansour, killing and wounding twenty-seven. Wasfi, who lives a stone's throw away, was shaken up. On an impulse, he had picked up his own weapon of choice—his cello—and sat in the middle of the scene of death, fire and desolation and played his own composition, 'Baghdad Mourning Melancholy'.

People gathered there, and shared a moment that can only be described as extraordinary. From soldiers to cleaners to shop owners, everyone stopped to listen. Even drivers stopped their cars in the middle of the road to partake in the moment of shared peace.

Since then, Wasfi has played at numerous other sites that have witnessed devastation. He hopes to one day play in Syria, a country he believes shares the pain that his country does.

'Hate is self-destructive,' Wasfi says. And he is challenging this destructive force of violence with a constructive one of creation. He believes that once people experience the positive effect of creation and construction, they will find violence unattractive.

The son of an Egyptian mother and an Iraqi father, Wasfi was born in Cairo and grew up in a musical family. He wants to use an art form he knows best—music—to bring about healing, cross-cultural integration, deradicalization and counterterrorism.

It is with the same belief that he founded the Peace Through Arts Global Foundation. The same intention led him to first play his cello in the ruins of terror in a video captured by his friend Amal Al Jubur. Sadly, Ammar Al Shahbander, a close friend of maestro Wasfi and Iraq director of the Institute for War and Peace Reporting, died only a few days after in another bomb site where a car detonated at Karrada district—where Wasfi had aimed to overcome the obstacles of terror and transcend through beauty.

What did Wasfi do? He grabbed his chair and cello and began to play at the site.

'When things are abnormal, we make things normal. We make things worth living for,' says Wasfi, looking into the distance, possibly imagining where else he can bring the normalcy of peace through the simple act of playing music.

50

The Rabbi of Kindness

ONE MAN'S EFFORT TO MAKE
KINDNESS VIRAL

Ottawa, Canada

Rabbi Reuven Bulka, aged seventy-seven, passed away on the fourth Sunday of June 2021 after a six-month-long battle with liver and pancreatic cancer.

But even in his final days, Rabbi Bulka was his cheerful self, doing what he did best— spreading kindness and joy to everyone around him—jesting with a nurse who asked if she could take his blood pressure, to which he replied that he would let her take it if only she would give it back!

It was this jolly nature and his lifelong endeavour to inspire people across the country to lead a humble and optimistic life devoted to kindness that conferred Ottawa's rabbi the nickname of 'Canada's Rabbi'. It was his life's purpose to make the world a better place.

Rabbi Bulka was born in London, England, and the family moved to the United States soon after the war. The son of a rabbi, Bulka received his rabbinic ordination in New York in 1965 and moved to Ottawa in 1967.

It was in Ottawa, in 2008, that Rabbi Bulka launched Kindness Week, empowering people in schools, workplaces and healthcare to embrace the values of kindness, such as empathy, respect, gratitude and compassion and working to build an everyday culture of kindness through community engagement, volunteerism and charity.

One of the most important questions that Rabbi Bulka believed one must ask oneself and as early as possible is, 'What can I do to make this world a better place?' A commitment to kindness, a core Jewish value, he believed, would make Canada a greater country and create a bigger impact on some of the critical issues it faces, including mental health, the cost of healthcare and bullying.

Kindness Week witnessed such an overwhelming response from the community that Rabbi Bulka and the team of Kind Canada, the not-for-profit organization Rabbi Bulka founded which grew out of this initiative to better integrate kindness in society, were inspired to introduce the kindness project across the country.

From the biggest act to the smallest gesture, Kind Canada has a kindness idea for everyone: collect books for your local library, eat lunch with a new colleague or schoolmate, return your shopping cart (and someone else's) to the cart stall, make a donation to your favourite charity, sign up for organ or tissue donation, donate blood (something Rabbi Bulka did 369 times!) and many more. Tools, guides, examples and research, the organization leaves you ready and excited for your journey of kindness.

In a process initiated by Rabbi Bulka, it was Senator Jim Munson who first wrote the 'Kindness Week' bill, which became law after it received Royal Assent in June 2021, with Kindness Week being celebrated in the third week of February every year in Canada. Munson credits Rabbi Bulka for building support among parliamentarians to get the private member's Kindness Bill through.

Whereas kindness encourages values such as empathy, respect, gratitude and compassion;

Whereas kind acts lead to the improved health and well-being of Canadians;

Whereas Kindness Week is already celebrated in some Canadian cities;

Whereas designating and celebrating a Kindness Week throughout Canada will encourage acts of kindness, volunteerism and charitable giving to the benefit of all Canadians;

Whereas Kindness Week will connect individuals and organizations to share resources, information and tools to foster more acts of kindness;

And whereas Parliament envisions that Kindness Week might encourage a culture of kindness in Canada throughout the year.

Ottawa Mayor Jim Watson, who also worked closely with Rabbi Bulka, said that the rabbi epitomized kindness.

And even now, the man continues to inspire kindness through the many lives he's touched who continue his legacy personally and are collectively, in the way of the Rabbi Bulka Kindness Project, dedicated to doing what he set out to do—making kindness go viral.

IN A GENTLE WAY, YOU CAN SHAKE THE WORLD

Mahatma Gandhi

BE KIND

Michael Blumenthal
(United States)

Not merely because Henry James said
there were but four rules of life—
be kind be kind be kind be kind—but
because it's good for the soul, and,
what's more, for others; it may be
that kindness is our best audition
for a worthier world, and, despite
the vagueness and uncertainty of
its recompense, a bird may yet wander
into a bush before our very houses,
gratitude may not manifest itself in deeds
entirely equal to our own, still there's
weather arriving from every direction,
the feasts of famine and feasts of plenty
may yet prove to be one, so why not
allow the little sacrificial squinches and
squigulas to prevail? Why not inundate
the particular world with minute particulars?
Dust's certainly all our fate, so why not
make it the happiest possible dust,
a detritus of blessedness? Surely
the hedgehog, furling and unfurling

into its spiked little ball, knows something
that, with gentle touch and unthreatening
tone, can inure to our benefit, surely the wicked
witches of our childhood have died and,
from where they are buried, a great kindness
has eclipsed their misdeeds. Yes, of course,
in the end so much comes down to privilege
and its various penumbras, but too much
of our unruly animus has already been
wasted on reprisals, too much of the
unblessed air is filled with smoke from
undignified fires. Oh, friends, take
whatever kindness you can find
and be profligate in its expenditure:
It will not drain your limited resources,
I assure you, it will not leave you vulnerable
and unfurled, with only your sweet little claws
to defend yourselves, and your wet little noses,
and your eyes to the ground, and your little feet.

* Curated by *The Alipore Post*

About Our Kindness Collaborators

The Heartfulness Institute

The Heartfulness Institute was founded with the vision of promoting inner excellence in individuals that leads to societal change. The Heartfulness relaxation and meditation practices regulate the mind and open the heart, so that change is possible and within the grasp of the individual. Heartfulness recognizes that the spiritual journey of an individual is greatly enhanced when one's life is led simply and in tune with nature. This practice is offered as a pro bono service to one and all, from all sections of society through its network of more than 15,000 trainers worldwide.

The Heartfulness Institute is an affiliate of Shri Ram Chandra Mission (SRCM), a seventy-five-year-old spiritual organization spread across more than 100 countries with over 275 centres all over the world (250 such centres are in India). The institute is headquartered in the pristine Kanha Shanti Vanam campus near Hyderabad, Telangana. To know more, visit https://heartfulness.org/?fbclid=IwAR1Wy1WBYrr3pdW 70Kx5OydvoP2gIPD7FmMNqzrJ_BXRli0_hAAwRGHJZHw.

faze media

Faze Media

Faze Media is a communications and media company based in Toronto, Canada. Since its launch as a national print magazine in 2000, Faze has been a positive and empowering community for young women. It connects with its readers through insightful and inspiring conversations around relevant and meaningful issues, sharing messages online, across social media, in print and face-to-face at live events. To know more, visit www.faze.ca.

GOODNET
GATEWAY TO DOING GOOD

Goodnet

Goodnet, part of the Arison Group, is an organization that connects people around the world with stories about doing good and spreading positivity. They created and manage the Goodnet online hub to promote written and video content linked to helping make the world a better place.

Since businesswoman and philanthropist, Shari Arison, initiator of 'Good Deeds Day', founded Goodnet in 2011, the team has put eyes and ears across the world to find and amplify the various ways the global community is doing good. They produce content that highlights sustainability, volunteering, charity work, green tech, mindful living, spirituality and more. Their mission is to share the good things happening globally, and they are proud to have fostered a vibrant and engaging social media and reader community committed to helping them spread positivity.

They believe that doing good is a state of mind, and it can accompany every action and shine through every thought. Goodnet believes that, as Shari puts it, 'A critical mass of people who want good, think good, speak good and do good can generate positive transformation worldwide.'

Visit them at www.goodnet.org/.

The Alipore Post

The Alipore Post is a weekly newsletter and online journal by Rohini Kejriwal that celebrates contemporary art, poetry, photography, music and all things creative.

Curated with love. Designed to inspire.

Newsletter: thealiporepost.substack.com
Journal: www.thealiporepost.com
IG: www.instagram.com/thealiporepost

References

Chapter 7: A Town of Two

- https://www.goodnewsnetwork.org/two-men-live-in-fukushima-taking-care-of-animals-naoto-matsumura/
- http://ganbarufukushima.blog.fc2.com/?fbclid=IwAR39Hj3IawdDOlp6RdWMnyqolFCKwhamsiB5U47da6S-4-0xp-O4WYWY-0o
- https://www.boredpanda.com/fukushima-radioactive-disaster-abandoned-animal-guardian-naoto-matsumura/
- https://allthatsinteresting.com/naoto-matsumura
- https://penntoday.upenn.edu/news/alone-again-fukushima
- https://www.youtube.com/watch?v=1lM9MIM_9U4&feature=emb_imp_woyt
- https://www.zmescience.com/other/feature-post/fukushima-animals-radioactive/
- https://www.timesnownews.com/the-buzz/article/meet-sakae-kato-man-in-jaoan-who-stayed-back-in-fukushima-nuclear-zone-to-take-care-of-abandoned-cats/728503
- https://www.reuters.com/article/us-japan-fukushima-anniversary-pets-wide-idUSKCN2AV2XO
- https://www.theguardian.com/artanddesign/gallery/2021/mar/05/the-man-who-saves-cats-in-fukushimas-nuclear-zone-in-pictures

Chapter 10: One with the River

- https://geographical.co.uk/places/wetlands/item/4076-the-goldman-environmental-prize-an-interview-with-recipient-maida-bilal
- https://www.earthisland.org/journal/index.php/articles/entry/the-river-is-part-of-me/

Chapter 13: Bibliomotocarro

- https://educated-traveller.com/2019/02/06/the-smallest-library-in-italy/
- https://www.ted.com/talks/antonio_la_cava_taking_the_culture_to_the_limits/transcript?language=en
- https://thevalemagazine.com/2018/12/22/antonio-la-cava-teacher-mobile-library-italy/
- https://www.bbc.com/culture/article/20190125-the-tiny-library-bringing-books-to-remote-villages

Chapter 14: Healing Together

- https://www.unhcr.org/news/stories/2020/10/5f8035a84/rohingya-refugee-children-learn-support.html
- https://www.thedailystar.net/opinion/news/together-we-heal-learn-and-shine-2114061

Chapter 20: Scouting for Joy

- https://www.goodnewsnetwork.org/russian-orphan-builds-playground/
- https://www.baltimoresun.com/news/bs-xpm-2009-01-11-0901100086-story.html
- https://www.broadleafpartners.com/2010/04/13/another-sign-of-the-times-eagle-scout-projects-go-global/

- https://edition.cnn.com/SPECIALS/cnn.heroes/archive09/alex.griffith.html
- https://betheanswerforchildren.wordpress.com/2009/09/10/griffith-chosen-as-a-cnn-hero/

Chapter 31: The Forest Warrior
- https://www.bbc.com/news/world-latin-america-57427697
- https://www.youtube.com/watch?v=K-3Qr4ztXZI
- https://www.oneearth.org/environmental-hero-liz-chicaje-churay/
- https://www.theguardian.com/environment/2021/jun/15/we-need-real-change-japanese-activist-urges-faster-coal-phase-out

Chapter 33: Rapping to Freedom
- https://www.sonita.net/
- https://asiasociety.org/asia-game-changers/sonita-alizadeh
- https://time.com/collection/next-generation-leaders/5277970/sonita-alizadeh-next-generation-leaders/
- https://www.rollingstone.com/culture/culture-features/how-afghan-rapper-sonita-alizadehs-song-brides-for-sale-changed-her-fate-198272/
- https://psmag.com/news/meet-afghanistans-youngest-female-rapper
- https://www.globalcitizen.org/en/content/this-girls-powerful-rap-saved-her-from-child-marri/?template=next
- https://www.theguardian.com/film/2016/mar/05/sonita-review-afghan-female-rapper-documentary
- https://edition.cnn.com/2015/10/11/world/afghanistan-rapper-sonita-alizadeh/index.html

Chapter 41: The Ones That Walked with Mammoths

- https://www.youtube.com/watch?v=mm2-tJHBFDw
- https://www.isa-germany.com/en/introduction-of-olya-esipova/
- https://www.wcnexpo.org/saiga
- https://baku-magazine.com/conservation/conservation-corner-saiga-alliance/
- http://saiga-conservation.org
- https://www.global-changemakers.net/post/olya-esipova-uzbekistan

Chapter 45: A Rose Is a Rose Is a Rose

- https://www.positive.news/society/democracy/roses-of-peace-bloom-in-nepal/
- https://ilepfederation.org/flower-power-how-roses-have-become-a-powerful-weapon-in-the-battle-against-stigma/
- https://www.giraffe.org/sushil-koirala